CONTENTS

D1232062

FOREWORD

Don't make your prayer a job. It's a gift. Don't make it a grim and costly ticket you must buy in order to gain admittance to the divine love—you're already there.

When you begin to exercise it's hard. You don't feel well. You don't like to sweat. Moving hurts. Everyone else is stronger and faster and looks better. You know that years of not moving have been bad for you, and now you feel like you're being punished for it. But you keep going.

And soon you begin to feel different. Wonderful. Soon you love to move, even love to sweat, soon your body loves it—it's what your body's made to do. Soon you feel strong. Soon you don't care what other people look like. Soon you don't feel guilty any more—you're doing good things for the body God gave you, and you're being blessed every time you do them.

Spiritual discipline is just like that. It can be hard at first. You can feel guilty and inadequate at first. I should have been praying and reading scripture already, you think. I don't do this right. Other people do it better.

But prayer's what you're created to do. You are naturally good at it—God made you that way. Soon you don't care what other people do, how long they've been doing it, whether they're better at it than you are. Soon you just love it for its own sake. Soon you hardly remember what made you feel guilty about it.

If you have trouble with the word "discipline," you won't later on—not after you get going in a routine that blesses you. In the meantime, use the word "practice." It's the same thing.

Advent

SUNDAY, ADVENT I

Pss 146, 147 * 111, 112, 113
Amos 1:1–5, 13–2:8
1 Thessalonians 5:1–11
Luke 21:5–19

Therefore encourage one another and build up
each other, as indeed you are doing.
I THESSALONIANS 5:11

Just a few weeks until the end of the quarter—financial people work overtime at this time of year and weeks into the new one to close everything out. This is hard—the family wants their attention, extra attention, right now. Shopping and decorating and cooking special foods. They daydream of naps the way other people daydream of sailboats.

Teachers unanimously report that the kids are off the wall during these weeks: excited about the holidays, unable to concentrate, titillated earlier and earlier each year by the toy manufacturers' television seductions. They're counting the days, the kids—and so are their teachers. And they, too, have families who want their attention, want the creativity they bring to the classroom to spill graciously into their own homes: beautiful decorations, wonderful presents, perfect cookies.

Psychotherapists say that this is a hard time of year: everyone's Norman Rockwell dreams of family once again dashed on the rocks of real life. *Why can't I stop trying to make my family like the Waltons?* a client wonders aloud, and the therapist sits in her chair and silently wonders the same thing about herself. Experienced as she is with other peoples' troubles, she stumbles into impossible dreams sometimes herself. *You'd think I'd know better,* she tells a colleague ruefully.

But it's not what we know. It's what we hope. That for which we long. Few things in life are stronger than hope, and few things hurt as much when they are dashed.

We have a Companion in our hope. And at the end of our hope here on the earth. Life is imperfect and then it ends, but our hope is not misplaced, even so. Our Companion will stay with us, and will lead us into the place where hope lives forever, never dashed, where there is no ruin. Quiet, perhaps discouraged, we light the first candle of Advent and, full of our need, prepare for him to come to us again.

MONDAY IN ADVENT I

Pss 1, 2, 3 * 4, 7
Amos 2:6–16
2 Peter 1:1–11
Matthew 21:1–11

"This is the prophet Jesus from Nazareth in Galilee."
MATTHEW 21:11

Many people don't know that Jesus appears in the Koran. But he does. The holy book of Islam says of Jesus just what the people of Jerusalem said when they first saw him: he was a prophet.

We say Jesus is the Son of God. But what do we mean by that? God's biological son? God's son by adoption, a holy man claimed by God as His very own son? Or God pretending to be human? We must confess that Jesus is the Son of God, we say, in order to be saved—but we cannot define for ourselves or for anyone else what that means. It is a reality beyond our reality, and a reality beyond any words we might suggest. Most spiritual realities are. They are mysterious to us by their very nature, and by the limits of our nature, as well.

So it's probably not a very good use of our time to tangle with each other for not believing the right thing about Jesus, since we can't arrive at much in the way of concrete truth about him. He is the Son of God, born into the human family, crucified for us and risen from the dead, and none of that requires our being able to define him. He is the one who challenged us to serve him by serving one another. Fighting about who he is uses precious time we could have spent doing this.

So much has been said and written about him that we think we know him. We even think we know what he looked like—long blond hair, kind blue eyes, tall and graceful, a long curly beard. That is, like a movie star. We even think we know what he thinks. He thinks what we think, doesn't he?

Usually, the prophets don't think just what we think. We wouldn't need them if they did. We can assume the Son of God isn't just like us, either—why have an Incarnation if the Messiah is just another one of us?

But he is one of us. And yet more. A prophet and healer—and more. A teacher and a preacher—and more. The Son of God, like no other before or since, from an existence in which there's no such thing as before or since. Just the eternal present of God.

TUESDAY IN ADVENT I

Pss 5, 6 * 10, 11
Amos 3:1–11
2 Peter 1:12–21
Matthew 21:12–22

*Do two walk together unless they
have made an appointment?*
AMOS 3:3

An ancient version of a saying we know better as "Where there's smoke, there's fire." The prophet isn't really a magic person who knows the future; he's just a person who can read signs everybody else sees, too. His denial system is out of order; he can't hide from things as well as the rest of us can. Can't and won't.

Most of our denial systems, on the other hand, are in perfect working condition. We are capable of overlooking very obvious dangers in order to believe that all is well and that the status quo will continue. Since we don't know how to change things, we easily talk ourselves into believing that things don't need changing.

What in your life is in obvious need of change and, at the same time, invisible to you? Am I able to smoke a pack of cigarettes a day and somehow think I won't get lung cancer or heart disease? Do I consume a six-pack of beer all by myself and tell myself I don't have a drinking problem because it's not hard liquor and I've never been fired from a job? Do I think my affair doesn't affect my marriage? Do I drive a gas-guzzling car and also tell myself I care about the environment?

If so, all of these things are probably obvious to everyone who sees me do them. I'm the only one who thinks they're hidden. I am like a small child who puts her hands in front of her eyes and thinks her mommy has disappeared.

And I will probably become angry at anyone who dares even mention any of them. The prophets always make people around them angry. That anger should be my first clue that something is wrong.

WEDNESDAY IN ADVENT I

Pss 119:1–24 * 12, 13, 14
Amos 3:12–4:5
2 Peter 3:1–10
Matthew 21:23–32

As the shepherd rescues from the mouth of the lion two legs, or a piece of an ear, so shall the people of Israel who live in Samaria be rescued, with the corner of a couch and part of a bed.
AMOS 3:12

It is hard for me to read this passage and others like it: I close my eyes and see the great pile of rubble where the towers of the World Trade Center once stood. I see chair legs and pieces of light fixtures, crushed paper cups and pieces of the metal panels that formed the outer skin of the buildings. I see unidentifiable bits of human flesh. For the most part, the recovery phase looked exactly like the rescue phase: only the name was different.

So this is rescue: there's nothing left here. Nothing here is in one piece. Nothing and nobody. We left the site and stopped at the decontamination station, where our boots were sprayed with water and something else before we walked away. What was that dust, I would wonder as I watched it swirl off my boots and into the gutter. What and who? I can never know. No one will ever know.

Given the right combination of exhaustion and grief, it was hard not to experience this suffering as punitive. What did this mean? What did we do to deserve this? What about those innocent people who were cooking, writing, making photocopies, doodling in meetings and riding the elevators that whooshed straight up 110 floors in about a minute? We must have done something terrible, to deserve all this.

But the moment such a thought entered my weary mind, I knew it could not be true. I know the people of ancient Israel thought that military victory and defeat were specific signs of God's favor or wrath, but I do not think so. Today I think God is present in the experience of the victims as well as of those who triumph over them. Today it is God's creating love I see everywhere, not God's whimsical or partisan "favor."

And the rescue? There are piles of rubble in life, more than we thought there were. They are not distributed fairly. No one escapes forever. And God works beside the rescuers, those who claw desperately through the wreckage in hopes of bringing somebody out alive.

THURSDAY IN ADVENT I

Pss 18:1–20 * 18:21–50
Amos 4:6–13
2 Peter 3:11–18
Matthew 21:33–46

So also our beloved brother Paul wrote to you according to the wisdom given him, speaking of this as he does in all his letters. There are some things in them hard to understand, which the ignorant and unstable twist to their own destruction, as they do the other scriptures.

2 PETER 3:15–16

So it's "our beloved brother Paul," eh? We know that there was actually little love lost between them—Peter and James on one side and Paul on the other represent the two poles of an intense rivalry in the early church: Do we accept non-Jews into the fellowship without requiring them to observe Jewish law? We know that Paul was jealous of Peter and James' status as apostles who had actually known Jesus when he walked the earth, as Paul did not. We see him, in his letters, struggling to get along with the folks in Jerusalem, collecting money for their widows and orphans, prevailing upon the members of his gentile churches to contribute to the welfare of these widows and orphans they would never meet—not always an easy sell. And we know that, in the end, it was Paul's view that prevailed: Christians don't keep kosher laws today, nor do we require circumcision. The community in Jerusalem would not remain the center of the faith.

And so this letter named for Peter remembers an amity that did not exist—it is probably written by someone who knew neither Peter nor Paul, and who lived after they both had died. We know that it was important to the early Church to believe that peace and love was universal among its members—but that human beings in community usually tussle with each other a bit here and there, and people who are involved with important things frequently disagree considerably about them.

So the early Church was inspired by imagined love and peace among the revered founders of their faith. And we are inspired by remembering that we moderns are not the only ones who quarrel. One way or another, each age gets what it needs from the study of scripture.

FRIDAY IN ADVENT I

Pss 16, 17 * 22
Amos 5:1–17
Jude 1–16
Matthew 22:1–14

Fallen, no more to rise, is maiden Israel. . . .
AMOS 5:2

Israel is sometimes imagined as a virgin: marriageable, a young girl with her life in front of her. Unspoiled, uncompromised—as yet. But foolish—vulnerable to the disastrous results of her own mistakes. The fall of such a one, a person who has not yet fully lived, who has not yet—and now will never—acquire wisdom, was among the saddest things Amos could imagine.

I think we can all agree on that—Amos is talking about the death of a child as a model for the tragedy of Israel's vanquishing, and most people can reach no further than that in imagining tragedy. It is those who have lived life who should die, not those who haven't tasted it yet. The death of your mother or father can hit you hard— I remember being unable to imagine living without my mother— but it isn't abnormal. It happens to everyone. The death of a child is a completely different loss.

At meetings of The Compassionate Friends, the organization of parents whose children have died, people often talk about other people's reactions to their loss. They find that some of their friends simply cannot approach them, and literally disappear from their lives forever. They also find that some people they never thought much about at all turn out to be there as good listeners and caring friends. Tragedy makes and breaks relationships. It can go either way. God reaches to human beings through the events of our history. God is always reaching for us, I think, and we always have the chance to reach back. We never *don't* have it. Even scary Amos knows that.

SATURDAY IN ADVENT I

Pss 20, 21:1–7 (8-14) * 110:1–5 (6–7), 116, 117
Amos 5:18–27
Jude 17–25
Matthew 22:15–22

*. . . as if someone fled from a lion,
and was met by a bear . . .*
AMOS 5:19

This always reminds me of cartoons from the 1950s: one cute furry animal pitted against another, each enduring attack and counterattack, falling off mountains, hurtling through brick walls and leaving behind holes shaped like their own bodies, being flattened by enormous falling rocks. And then there they are, in the next frame, up and ready for battle again. The cartoon animals always recovered, so their injuries were slapstick—we laughed. Nothing bad stuck to them. They were always okay.

The day of the Lord is different, Amos warns. Take it seriously. You think you've got life under control because you're religiously observant? Life is not under control. Not ever. Anything can happen. Run from a lion and a bear gets you. A real lion. A real bear.

We watch cartoon disasters and, if we are not careful, we cease to believe in the possibility of real ones. We saw faraway horrors on the television and didn't think it could happen here—white Americans were stunned that the World Trade Center could have been bombed deliberately. Surprised. Black Americans, shaken and saddened by the bombing also, were less surprised. They already knew that people could do terrible things to other people they didn't even know. On purpose.

How to protect ourselves? Set up a Commission to study the bombing and our preparedness. Make changes in our intelligence gathering, in our managing of airport security. Do what you can—but don't be surprised if all your preparation cannot avert every disaster. People who want to hurt other people will find a way to do so.

Are such terrible days the day of the Lord? Was 9/11 the day of the Lord? I think not. It was a day of human horror and human hatred, not of divine retribution. The Lord was present in it, not in the person and bitter vision of the terrorists but in the wounded but powerful love that gathered in the wreckage they left behind.

SUNDAY, ADVENT II

Pss 148, 149, 150 * 114, 115
Amos 6:1–14
2 Thessalonians 1:5–12
Luke 1:57–68

They said to her, "None of your relatives has this name."
LUKE 1:61

Naming your baby assumes great importance as you prepare for her. Or maybe you prepare for a *him*. Should you name your baby after your parents? After yourself? After a famous person? Somehow certain baby names become common in different eras—many of my mother's friends were named Betty, but I have only one contemporary with that name. Jasons and Joshuas and Maxes, Tiffanies and Briannas abound today, but none of my adult friends are named Tiffany or Brianna.

Barbara has never been a common name. Truth to tell, I have always disliked it. *Well, why don't you change your name, then?* My friend asked me once. *It's important to like your name.*

Is it? I've never liked mine, but I don't know that it's slowed me down any in life, and I can't imagine changing it. This disliked name is part of who I am, a minor cross to bear—the first of many more important ones.

Well, what name would you choose if you could choose? Q wants to know.

I don't know, I tell him. And, of course, I *can* choose. Even though I dislike it, I haven't proposed an alternative. It's just my name.

A new name for Zachariah and Elizabeth's new baby. A name nobody else had. A new name for a unique new person, someone who does unexpected things even before he's born: a baby who recognizes the unborn Messiah from the womb. Something new is coming, and we no longer need to be confined by what has always been. He's not named for his dad. Or for anyone else in his family. They can't lead him into the new places he will be called to go. *His name is John.*

MONDAY IN ADVENT II

Pss 25 * 9, 15
Amos 7:1–9
Revelation 1:1–8
Matthew 22:23–33

"How can Jacob stand? He is so small!"
AMOS 7:2

Not once but *twice*, Amos poses this rhetorical question: Israel as a toddler, a child too young to understand that his behavior is wrong. We are children, foolish like children—don't leave us because of our sin. Stay with us and help us to stand.

Is it really true that we don't know of our own sinfulness? Sometimes. We don't always see our self-absorption for what it is, so effectively do we clothe it as something else—we usually find a way to believe things we want are in the general interest, as well. Most political speech asserts this claim—the legislation that benefits me directly will also, magically, benefit you. I just can't say *how* right now.

And sometimes our sin is more outright—we are exploitative of others and we know it, but we want the fruits of our sin more, I guess, than we want the more godly satisfactions of virtue and self-control. This, too, is like a toddler, but not the innocent kind—it's like the toddler who hides when you come upon him engaged in a forbidden activity. He thinks he's in the clear if you don't catch him.

Amos pleads for God's patient presence in our growing process. Don't go. Wait until we get the point; don't leave us before them.

Okay. I will stay. But listen to what your life is teaching you. Take from it even the hard lessons it will hand you—for if you do not, life will hand you harder ones still.

TUESDAY IN ADVENT II

Pss 26, 28 * 36, 39
Amos 7:10–17
Revelation 1:9–16
Matthew 22:34–46

"I am no prophet, nor a prophet's son; but I am a herdsman, and a dresser of sycamore trees. . . ."
AMOS 7:14

By the time Amos appeared, the position of prophet was well established in the kingdom of Israel. They were permanent civil servants, really. Being a prophet was more or less a career. Your job was to tell the king what God wants, so he could make his plans according to God's will.

Of course, the temptation to tell the king that God wanted what the king wanted must have been enormous. And powerful people don't always take bad news well: there was a major disincentive to deliver any prophecy suggesting that the king had somehow displeased the Almighty.

It is this enterprise from which the rustic Amos distances himself in verse 13. I'm not a professional. I don't make money prophesying. I'm a farmer, for heaven's sake. We are accustomed to claims of outsider status on the lips of political candidates—even candidates who have been members of Congress for decades try to find ways to call believably for change, as if they had not been part of the system themselves for years.

Amos probably didn't even need to say that. His message was unprofessional enough. A fierce and frightening call for repentance. What goes around will certainly come around, he says, and an exception will not be made in your case.

I hope my actions don't have consequences. I hope there's a special, impenetrable cloak of magic around me that preserves me from the effects of my own error and selfishness. That's what I hope. But I know that it is not so. Better clean up my act while I still can.

WEDNESDAY IN ADVENT II

Pss 38 * 119:25–48
Amos 8:1–14
Revelation 1:17–2:7
Matthew 23:1–12

"The scribes and the Pharisees sit on Moses' seat; therefore,
do whatever they teach you and follow it; but do not do
as they do, for they do not practice what they teach."
MATTHEW 23:2–3

Do as I say, not as I do! my dance teacher used to tell us ruefully, groaning as she attempted to demonstrate a new turn or a new combination. She was somewhere between forty and fifty years old, probably, and her well-trained body was becoming soft and undependable.

She had a hot temper, and embarrassed me many times in front of the other students when I failed at something. I loved ballet so much that only once did I let her drive me away, though, and then only for a little while. I couldn't go elsewhere; she was the only ballet teacher in that small town.

The scribes and the Pharisees were the only show in town, too. They held the power—they sat in the Moses seat, the bench in every synagogue on which the person who interpreted the law sat while he did so. Don't let their failings drive you away from their teachings, Jesus says. Do as they say, not as they do.

All of us are unable to fulfill the law. Even those of us whose efforts are wholehearted inevitably fall short, and most of us lose the thread of even the effort, and lose it frequently. No human example of goodness will suffice every time. No matter how much you love and respect your role model, he or she is a mere human being.

None of our failures invalidate the rightness of what we know to be true. It's common for a teenager to imagine that he has *discovered* hypocrisy, that he is the first to realize that people are sometimes less than they seem, that they fall short of what they claim. He is horrified and righteously indignant—until he accumulates a little mileage himself, and finds his own performance falling short of his own virtue sometimes. Oh, he thinks. I didn't know that everyone falls short. I thought it was just my dad.

It's not just dad. Or mom. Or the president. It's everyone. We're still responsible for finding out the right course and struggling to stay on it, even when we know we're going to fail sometimes. We don't have to be hypocrites. Not as long as we can be honest about the failures we share with everyone else.

THURSDAY IN ADVENT II

Pss 37:1–18 * 37:19–42
Amos 9:1–10
Revelation 2:8–17
Matthew 23:13–26

For you tithe mint, dill, and cummin, and have neglected the weightier matters of the law: justice and mercy and faith. It is these you ought to have practiced without neglecting the others.
MATTHEW 23:23

Some weird stuff used to come into the food pantry at St. Clement's sometimes—olives stuffed with garlic cloves, fancy tins of anchovies, special little boxes of imported tea bags, jars of exotic preserves. When enough of the oddities accumulated, we'd put one in each of the first fifty or so bags, as an extra item. I don't know what the people did with them when they got home. I hope they enjoyed them.

I suspect that these delicacies were "re-gifted" to us—things that people got in a fruit basket at Christmas, or that somebody who didn't know them very well brought as a hostess gift. I don't think anybody stood in the grocery store and asked herself, *Now, which shall I buy to give to the poor? The anchovies or the olives?* These things were extra things. Things they didn't want anyway.

Nothing wrong with a garlic-stuffed olive. Garlic is good for you, and so are olives. It's certainly better to give it away than to let it gather dust on a New York kitchen shelf—few people in the city have pantries, for space is a very precious thing there. But we have a higher calling than that of giving away things we don't want anyway. More intention is asked of us. The poor need and deserve more than our leftovers.

Probably we should give to the poor first, not last. Before we've done the things we want to do and run out of money. We should put them first, so we don't forget them, and trust God to take care of us. So that our leftovers don't end up being all we have to give.

FRIDAY IN ADVENT II

Pss 31 * 35
Haggai 1:1–15
Revelation 2:18–29
Matthew 23:27–39

But I have this against you: you tolerate that woman Jezebel, who calls herself a prophet and is teaching and beguiling my servants to practice fornication and to eat food sacrificed to idols.
REVELATION 2:20

The moment we see the name Jezebel, the least biblically literate among us knows immediately that nothing good will follow. Was the "Jezebel" of Revelation an actual woman, styling herself a prophet and preaching heresy? Maybe. Or was the "woman" Jezebel a rival church, one of the Gnostic communities that threatened the fragility of early orthodoxy? Maybe. It was a long time ago. None of us were around.

Whichever it was, we can't miss the passion of the writer. These matters were of enormous emotional importance to him. Controversies we can no longer even understand troubled him deeply. The list of early heresies is long. Their names are even longer. Most of them have been forgotten by almost everybody—only a few scholars remember. But people were angry and frightened about them once. Some people even killed for their version of the truth.

People want to read the book of Revelation, struggle through it with their calculators in their hands, attempting to scale its strange mathematics. They think it contains secret knowledge about the end of the world, and that maybe they can get the jump on some important things if they just figure it out.

But Revelation tells us more about the world of the first-century church than it tells us about the end of time—about what they feared, what they loved and what they hated, what they expected, how they imaged things in their vivid imaginations. They were aflame with zeal for their faith, and convinced—as many of their descendants are also convinced—that their local understanding of God's action was the only possible one. It is in this that we are most their descendents, not in their visions of strange heavenly beasts and frightening hellish ones, powerful luminous virgins and dangerous bloody whores, but in the essential narrowness of our vision where God is concerned. They turned their eyes inward to their own lurid imaginations, and what they saw could be monstrous. We turn our eyes inward to ourselves and we become monstrous, too. Turn outward, upward, open your heart and mind fully to just how majestic and just how loving our God is, and all the monsters disappear.

SATURDAY IN ADVENT II

Pss 30, 32 * 42, 43
Haggai 2:1–9
Revelation 3:1–6
Matthew 24:1–14

And because of the increase of lawlessness,
the love of many will grow cold.
MATTHEW 24:12

We grow into that which our culture permits—or perhaps we shrink into it. Just a glance back a few decades demonstrates this: So many things nobody would have countenanced in the 1950s are commonplace today. We are more profane, more violent, more cynical, and more entitled, much less apt to inconvenience ourselves for any reason. Much less apt to think we have an obligation to do so.

So were the 1950s a golden age? The 40s? No. They shrank to fit the limits of their culture, too—the racially segregated schools, restaurants, public spaces they took for granted would shock us today. The glaring inequality between men and women in those days was not glaring to them. We see it now, from our distance. We see *them*, but it's hard to see ourselves.

Maybe each age has its own lovelessness, its own ways of retreating from the humanity of others. But maybe each age also has its own courage, something that bears remembering when we lose patience with the sins peculiar to our own. What do we do well? What have we found—or perhaps, are just beginning to find—that was missed before? I can think of a few things—a recognition that our wealth has a cost to others, that the environment needs care. That children have rights beyond those derived from the rights of their parents. You can think of others.

For better or for worse, we don't live in another time. We live now. Perhaps our culture does sag below its desired mark, far below what it might be. But nothing says we have to sag with it.

SUNDAY, ADVENT III

Pss 63:1–8 (9–11), 98 * 103
Amos 9:11–15
2 Thessalonians 2:1–3, 13–17
John 5:30–47

*"You search the scriptures, because you think that in them
you have eternal life, and it is they that testify on my behalf.
Yet you refuse to come to me to have life."*
JOHN 5:39–40

Sometimes we try to imprison Jesus in the scriptures, bind him to their time and place and worldview, as if he were the Lord of the era of their composition but not of our own. Protective of the book, we will not allow him to do anything that isn't in it. We can see plainly that the spirit of God moved through several very different cultures during the course of the scriptures' composition—a nomadic one, an agrarian one, a theocracy, a monarchy—and through different kinds of families—polygamous families were the norm in the earlier books of the Old Testament, an arrangement that had disappeared in Judaism by the time of Jesus. Slavery was part of normal social organization in most of scripture, although how a person got to be a slave varied from age to age. It's pretty hard to do what so many earnest people want so much to do: to order our lives, literally, according to the scriptures. Well, *which* scriptures? we'd find ourselves asking pretty quickly.

That is why we do not worship the Bible itself. It is the record of God's self-revealing to Israel and to the early Church. Just as often, it is also the record of each one getting the message all wrong. Sometimes it reports this openly. Other times, it embodies it, and we must figure it out on our own. Does the fact that the Israelites understood the destruction of the Egyptians at the Red Sea to be an act of God on their own behalf mean we should consider the death of our enemies to be God's will now? Most of us would think not. Now that story gives us another gift, a different gift from the one it gave its first readers. And we must work to get it—the story of the Egyptians at the Red Sea is a hard one for many modern readers.

What will do, in your life, what the things of which we read in sacred texts did in the lives of those who first wrote and first read them? How does God speak to us today, and how does our experience of God connect with our history? It's work, finding out, hard work, learning how to receive the gifts scripture gives us today. But it is good work, for we do it in the communion of the saints.

MONDAY IN ADVENT III

Pss 41, 52 * 44
Zechariah 1:7–17
Revelation 3:7–13
Matthew 24:15–31

"So when you see the desolating sacrilege standing in the holy place, as was spoken of by the prophet Daniel . . ."
MATTHEW 24:15

We are told by some scholars that the Romans caused a statue of the emperor to be erected in the temple at Jerusalem—although others say that such a provocation would have been an unlikely move on the part of the practical politicians of Rome. Whichever view is correct, the writer of the gospel of Matthew believed it. That's what the "desolating sacrilege" was: this statue of a human being claiming divinity, right in the place where the God who cannot be represented was understood to be most present. It is hard to imagine anything more calculated to humiliate the Jews than this.

Now, understand that Jesus is talking about a prophecy of Daniel, written before he himself walked the earth. And we know that the temple was destroyed forty years after the crucifixion of Jesus. So neither Jesus nor Daniel lived to see the statue erected in the temple, or its destruction—that happened later. And we know that Matthew writes sometime in the last quarter of the first century—maybe in the 80s: We know this in part because of lines like this that betray knowledge of what was to come. Jesus didn't see the temple destroyed and the dispersion of the Jewish community in Israel, and neither had Daniel. But Matthew did.

It had such a terrible effect on them. No temple worship, ever again—modern Jewish worship uses the prayer, song, scripture, and teaching of the law that took place in the synagogue, not the sacrifices offered in the temple. Those are gone for good. And no homeland—until the founding of the modern state of Israel, all Jews were, in a sense, wandering. Desolation, to be without a temple.

But Judaism was portable. It survived the loss of its centralized worship. Most people would say, in fact, that it was this very loss that saved it—if the temple had remained standing, the site of daily bloody sacrifices of sheep and birds, would the faith of the Jews have made it into the modern world? Deprived of this kind of worship, the Jews were thrown back upon the only kind of faith that could survive into modern times. The cults of Mithras, of Dionysius, of Diana, Mars—their temples were not destroyed by the Romans. They were destroyed by the march of time. Not one of them remains an active faith. We have outgrown them.

TUESDAY IN ADVENT III

Pss 45 * 47, 48
Zechariah 2:1–13
Revelation 3:14–22
Matthew 24:32–44

"From the fig tree learn its lesson: as soon as its branch becomes tender and puts forth its leaves, you know that summer is near."
MATTHEW 24:32

I guess it's dead, Q said, and his fig tree certainly looked dead: its long branches stubbornly bare, long after all the surrounding plants were a hopeful green.

Well, maybe we can get another one, I comforted. But a few days later, a surprise: a fringe of tiny green leaves around the crown of the roots.

So we chopped the dead branches to the ground and the new ones grew toward the sun, taller than their fallen predecessors. And their leaves grew, large and mitten-shaped, and soon the tiny figs appeared, at the place where stem meets branch. Actual *figs*, in New Jersey.

The natural world signals its own future. Buds swell on branches. Young birds molt, making room for their adult feathers. Clouds gather before a storm. Cats grow heavy coats before the winter. Women's bellies swell, and everyone knows a baby's on the way.

Does the spiritual life signal its own tomorrow? Can you tell what's ahead by looking around you now? The moral life certainly does, and the realm of politics, as well; in each of those worlds, consequences follow actions as night follows day, and there is no such thing as a free lunch. But what of the deep recesses of the spirit where prayer lives?

We take the signs of our spirits' future, often, as signs of defeat. Prayer goes dry on us, becomes a joyless chore, and we think we have lost our connection with God. Not so: We have only received an advisory about a coming change. Time to wake up and see what other place God might inhabit in you besides the one he always visits. What other practice might work new muscles in your soul?

We have many ways of praying, and the cessation of one means that it's time for another to begin.

WEDNESDAY IN ADVENT III

Pss 119:49–72 * 49, (53)
Zechariah 3:1–10
Revelation 4:1–8
Matthew 24:45–51

But if that wicked slave says to himself, "My master is delayed,"
and he begins to beat his fellow-slaves, and eats and drinks with
drunkards, the master of that slave will come on a day when he does
not expect him and at an hour that he does not know.
MATTHEW 24:48–50

Why does the death penalty not deter crime? Why has the crime rate not gone down in states where it is enthusiastically applied? Why don't wrongdoers stop and think about what might happen to them if they're caught?

Simple: Criminals never think they *will* be caught.

The wicked servant thinks his master's delay gives him infinite opportunity to pursue his evil designs unmolested. But we don't have infinite opportunity for anything in this life, good or bad. All our chickens come home to roost sooner or later. Some of them are very late, but they will all return to us in the end.

So we should wipe from our minds the idea that external curbs on our baser instincts are the only ones that matter, or that there is any way to escape them. However they may delude themselves, criminals don't have very easy lives. They're apprehended and punished. They have to hide what they do. They can't tell anyone the truth, and so they can't really love anyone. Wrongdoing makes us profoundly lonely, and half the time we don't even know it.

Living in a different place is a happier thing: expecting a reckoning, expecting to be judged—but expecting to be judged by someone who is passionately on our side. Judged and helped to grow into who it is we're supposed to be. Then we're able to be honest about our mistakes and shortcomings, to bring them forward and show them forth in order to let God begin to heal and repair them.

THURSDAY IN ADVENT III

Pss 50 * (59, 60) or 33
Zechariah 4:1–14
Revelation 4:9–5:5
Matthew 25:1–13

*Then all those bridesmaids got up
and trimmed their lamps.*
MATTHEW 25:7

At first, you approach an oil lamp in what seems to you a reasonable way: The longer I make the wick, the more light I'll have, right? So you pull out a healthy length of wick and light it: indeed, it flames up gratifyingly. But soon the glass chimney of the lamp is black with the soot of it, and you have hardly any light at all. Your assumption was wrong: You need to keep your wick about a quarter of an inch long: light, but no smoke.

The wise virgins were wiser in all kinds of ways, I suppose, but the main one was in realizing that you have to plan ahead in life. Not everything can be done at the last minute, even if you are a person who works better under pressure.

The spiritual life is one of the things that takes time to settle in, so that it's ready whenever it is needed. You can't just come up with one in a moment of stress. This is not to say that God won't listen to your prayers if you haven't done your homework—God listens to everybody's prayers, and homework has nothing to do with it. It's we who need the comfort and stability of an ongoing spiritual preparation, not God.

At first, it sounds like the story of the wedding banquet is a story about homework and promptness, as if God had limited windows of opportunity to receive us. I think not. It's a story about us, really, more than one about God. Our unreadiness is our own, not God's. And that's really good news: It means that readiness can be ours, too, that we can prepare to receive the gift of God's presence in life, starting here, starting now.

FRIDAY IN ADVENT III

Pss 40, 54 * 51
Zechariah 7:8–8:8
Revelation 5:6–14
Matthew 25:14–30

"Well done, good and trustworthy slave . . ."
MATTHEW 25:21

This is what we want to hear from the boss: We did well. We did good work. We are acceptable. Most of us live for that praise.

You don't always get it, of course. There are bosses who never speak to you except when you've made a mistake. There are parents like that, too. It is disheartening for the one hungry for praise, and it has a curious effect, one that the powerful one did not intend: He thinks his criticism will instruct. Instead, it discourages. He thinks it will produce greater effort. Instead, it produces less.

Perfectionism is like that, curiously inverting its own desires. Because I cannot do something flawlessly, I decide not even to begin it. If I never finish it, I'll never have to read my bad reviews. I long to do things well, but I dare not even attempt them. I might get it wrong.

And so you sit in a messy house you hate because you know you won't clean it up perfectly. You stay in a job you hate because you don't think you can get the perfect job. You don't fall in love with anyone because everyone has something wrong with him. You eat most of a chocolate cake in the afternoon because you failed to follow your eating plan in the morning. You don't go to the gym because you didn't go yesterday and you've ruined your attendance record. What's the use of even trying? you say. I've ruined everything already.

But "ruined" and "not perfect" aren't synonyms. Nothing on this earth is perfect. And very little is really ruined.

SATURDAY IN ADVENT III

Pss 55 * 138, 139:1–17 (18–23)
Zechariah 8:9–17
Revelation 6:1–17
Matthew 25:31–46

"Truly I tell you, just as you did it to one of the least of these who are members of my family, you did it to me."
MATTHEW 25:40

There are many ingredients to a spiritual life—so many, in fact, that one person would not expect to exercise them all. Prayer, fasting, retreats, confession, journaling, centering, meditative walking, devotional reading, the study of scripture—people who begin to pay attention to their spiritual selves become hungry to learn about each of these things and to try some of them. Some of them are just not a good fit. But some of them are, and they become beloved.

We are apt to think of the spiritual life exclusively in terms of such inward-looking activities—things about ourselves and our interior relationship with God. But no spiritual life can be called either complete or Christian if it lacks contact with the world of those who suffer. We are not put here on earth simply to have an exquisite personal spirituality. The truth about the spiritual life and your own sense of well-being is this: Service to others is an integral part of it. If you are feeling lost and unsatisfied with your spiritual life, no matter what devotional tool you try, and you cannot point to some concrete way in which you regularly serve those less fortunate than yourself—that may well be the problem.

What's your prayer posture? Kneeling? Sitting? Like mine, sometimes—lying in a bathtub of lovely, sweet-smelling bubbles? Terrific—but if you are not also on your feet in the service of someone else, get there as soon as you can. It's probably what you've been missing.

SUNDAY, ADVENT IV

Pss 24, 29 * 8, 84
Genesis 3:8–15
Revelation 12:1–10
John 3:16–21

"Indeed, God did not send the Son into the world to condemn the world, but in order that the world might be saved through him."
JOHN 3:17

I *can't feel close to Jesus,* my friend says. *He makes me feel guilty. He died for my sins before I was even born. I feel like I killed him.* She likes the Holy Spirit instead—less biography.

She feels condemned by Jesus—by the Jesus who forgave even those who drove nails into his bare hands, at the very moment they were doing it. Feels that somehow he's not going to be able to handle her sins. Or maybe that he will handle them too well—she'll have to let them go, and she feels compelled to cling to them instead. And so Jesus makes her feel ashamed.

I never knew shame to be of much use to anyone. It seems mostly to act on us as a paralyzing agent: We can't move. Can't approach. Too convinced of our own worthlessness. Too certain that we should be able to move the heavy rock of it on our own, that it's wrong to ask for help. We'll do almost anything to change the subject. Such a long and intricate performance, the dance of self-justification. The story of why we don't need saving. The tale of why everything was someone else's fault.

And it feels so good when it stops. I don't have to justify myself at all. It's not horrible if I made mistakes, even big ones—it's expected. I'm a fallen being, like everyone else. I will have help in accomplishing what cleanup I can, help in embracing the sweet and surprising welcome of repentance, so different from the stolid isolation of shame. Before I even begin, Jesus invites me to it. While I'm still on the road, he meets me more than halfway.

MONDAY IN ADVENT IV

Pss 61, 62 * 112, 115
Zephaniah 3:14–20
Titus 1:1–16
Luke 1:1–25

*Since many have undertaken to set down an orderly account
of the events that have been fulfilled among us, just as they
were handed on to us by those who from the beginning were
eyewitnesses and servants of the word, I too decided, after
investigating everything carefully from the very first, to write
an orderly account for you, most excellent Theophilus, so that
you may know the truth concerning the things about
which you have been instructed.*

LUKE 1:1–4

We might rush through Luke's very courteous beginning: Enough of these opening pleasantries—hurry up and get to the story. But wait. There are some things to see here.

"Many have undertaken to compile a narrative," he says. There were many gospels written in the first century. The four enshrined in the Christian scriptures are not even the only ones that survive—another dozen or more can be read today, in English translation. Ours were just the ones that survived the final cut. Many people wanted to share the story, and those who could write did so—each with his own take on what had happened.

And Luke uses the phrase "set down." These aren't things Luke dreamed up—they are stories and teachings they had heard. Some were oral tradition. Some were written down, but have since been lost: Luke could read them, but we can no longer do so. They're passing on history, as far as Luke is concerned—that's why he wants to be sure we know that he heard much of what he heard from eyewitnesses.

And one more thing: he addresses his ornate preamble to "Theophilus." Literally, "God-lover." Perhaps it's coincidence; maybe that was just the man's name. Better scholars than I—a group that includes practically everybody—have written extensively about who Theophilus might have been: an eminent Roman, maybe, or perhaps a Jewish high priest. There was a high priest of that name in office shortly after the crucifixion. Maybe so.

But perhaps Luke is writing to us, to those in every age who walk the path of learning to recognize Christ where we see him, and to experience the love of God. Yes, I think so—even if he wasn't writing to us then, he is writing to us now.

TUESDAY IN ADVENT IV

Pss 66, 67 * 116, 117
1 Samuel 2:1b–10
Titus 2:1–10
Luke 1:26–38

Hannah prayed and said, "My heart exults in the Lord; my strength is exalted in my God."
1 SAMUEL 2:1

If this sounds familiar to Christians, it's because it was also familiar to young Mary, centuries after Hannah lived and died, when she sang what we now know as the Magnificat—it's just about the same song. God has acted on behalf of one who has been faithful, signaling the overturning of every power inequity that plagues humankind.

With all of our technical approaches to conception and childbearing—special hormone injections, alternative ways of encouraging the fertilization of eggs, implanting embryos, freezing spare ones—parents who struggle to conceive today know all too well that there is much outside of our control. It costs a fortune, and sometimes it doesn't work. But when it does, it is the same as every birth everywhere, in every time: a miracle. If this can be so for us, with all our sophisticated tools, what must it have been for barren Hannah, who had none of them? More than a miracle, if there is such a thing.

So frequently the birth of a miracle baby heralds the mighty acts of God in scripture. So many noble births happen in unusual circumstances—Jesus, to be sure, but Samuel, too. Samson. Jacob and Esau, Joseph. Moses. John the Baptist. Pay attention, these miracle babies tell us: God is about to act. Nothing about what you are about to hear is normal. It's all going to be extraordinary. It will all reveal God to you.

If we were reading Luke for the very first time, we wouldn't pay so much attention, so early, to Mary's story if she didn't give us a clue from Hannah's. But right away, we remember an ancient figure who had a special relationship with God from the beginning of his life. We hear her song, and we remember it. And we listen: Something important is about to happen.

WEDNESDAY IN ADVENT IV

Pss 72 * 111, 113
2 Samuel 7:1–17
Titus 2:11–3:8a
Luke 1:39–48a (48b–56)

*"My soul magnifies the Lord, and my
spirit rejoices in God my Savior. . . ."*
LUKE 1:46–47

And here is it: that which was foretold. Notice that there is absolutely nothing about the current state of things to suggest this: An unmarried girl in a small town in an occupied country finds herself inexplicably pregnant. She is not sure her fiance will accept her once he learns her secret. This could cost her life, and it certainly will cost her reputation.

Rule number one about Jesus: Don't judge a book by its cover. Very little about him is as one would think it should be for the Son of God.

And yet Mary rejoices as if God had redeemed Israel already. As if everything had been accomplished. She cannot have known the future—her practical question "How can this be?" confirms that. But she knows what trust is.

As we follow her through her brief centrality in the Jesus story, she is quiet after she sings this song. She is thinking. Visitors come to see her baby, and she receives them quietly: They leave with loud rejoicing, and she remains quiet—Luke says she "ponders." The events in her life have given her much to ponder already, and she is still young.

How does the world look? Redeemed? It still does not. But don't rush to conclusions. Remain quiet and observe. Ponder what you see. Our story isn't finished yet.

THURSDAY IN ADVENT IV

Pss 80 * 146, 147
2 Samuel 7:18–29
Galatians 3:1–14
Luke 1:57–66

Then King David went in and sat before the Lord,
and said, "Who am I, O Lord God, and what is my house,
that you have brought me thus far?
2 SAMUEL 7:18

Every famous person was once unknown. They seem to us to carry the seeds of their celebrity from birth: We look at pictures of them as children, and it seems to us that they knew they would be great one day. But they didn't know, not then and not now. They don't think they're particularly great, most of them—and one tires quickly of the ones who do.

Great gifts, even gifts that have been honed by years of study and hard work, once-in-a-century gifts, once-in-a-millennium gifts, like Mozart's, come from somewhere else. They are gifts: However hard we work, we cannot manufacture greatness. A certain workmanlike competence is the most we can summon on our own.

I have always thought that it must be for this reason that we are given some stories about great figures like David that put him in a bad light—he is an adulterer, a murderer. He is immodest. It is as if the writer were going out of his way to show us that David is far from perfect. Why tell us these unsavory things, if you want us to think that David was a superman? But that's not what the writer wants. Not a superman. Just a man whom God chose and endowed with the gifts he would need for the task he was given.

There's a reason why you have what you have, a reason beyond your own enjoyment. You're here for a reason. Why did God give you and not somebody else the gifts you have? Because it's you he wants to use them. What are they? Find out. Where are you supposed to use them? Ask. Who are you, and why has God brought you this far?

FRIDAY IN ADVENT IV

Pss 93, 96 * 148, 150
Baruch 4:21–29
Galatians 3:15–22
Luke 1:67–80 or Matthew 1:1–17

My pampered children have traveled rough roads. . . .
BARUCH 4:26

If you are reading this, it's because Christmas Eve is on a Saturday this year, and Sunday is Christmas Day—the second deadliest of combinations for altar guilds, organists, choir members, florists, and parish priests. (Absolute deadliest is when Christmas Eve is on a Sunday, and you have all the morning services and then one or two or even three in the evening as well. Heavy church. And Christmas Day? Talk about quiet.)

I thought of this yesterday, when I upset an entire carafe of water on the freshly ironed fair linen in the chapel during the healing service. Only one altar guild member was present, and she was kindness itself, bundling up the wet cloth and taking it home to iron, in a week when I know she has precious little time for the unnecessary duplication of ironing. I have something of a reputation in that parish: Once, when I was a young curate there, I spilled most of a cruet of *red wine* on the snowy fair linen.*

Ed Chinery came over last evening at five o'clock to get some ivy—*Take all you want,* I said, and we went out with a flashlight in the solstice dark, pulling up long ropes of the glossy leaves until Ed's arms were full of them. He came from a long day at work. When he left, the church was exquisite. The altar guild is magic like that. Miracle workers.

We say it is heavy church for us, the clergy. But we have taken vows to be there and do this work—the others who labor so hard to make the church wonderful come from busy homes, draining jobs, and they don't have to be there. They could stay home. It is the goodness of their hearts and their love of the community that brings them out on a dark night to create beauty to the glory of God, that sends them home with a bundle of damp linen, when they thought all the ironing was done, to make it crisp and perfect—again.

I wonder if they know how redemptive their work is? How silently eloquent the crisp white of the fair linen, the perfect squares of the purificators, the gleam of the silver and brass, how these things speak of a restored human nature, of the rough places leveled and straightened, of all the stains of human life on earth removed in Christ? Do they know that the holly and the ivy promise resurrection to the people of God in the depths of winter, and that these physical things speak volumes to the people who will appear on Christmas Eve but not at other times, who don't think about God much during the year, that these beauties may touch them more deeply than any priest's sermon?

---

*You may or may not know that my repeated use of "fair linen" is not just a poetic turn of phrase on my part: It is a technical term for the white cloth that covers the altar. Caring for one is not for sissies—I can remember my mother down on her hands and knees on the rug, ironing the fair linen on a triple layer of clean sheets. The poetry comes from the sixteenth century, not from me. When you say it, you say *"fair* linen," emphasizing the first word. Just a little church trivia, should you ever need it.

CHRISTMAS EVE

Pss 45, 46 * 89:1–29
Baruch 4:36–5:9 * Isaiah 59:15b–21
Galatians 3:23–4:7 * Philippians 2:5–11
Matthew 1:18–25

And he named him Jesus.
MATTHEW 1:25

Each ginger bear has two round currant eyes and a round currant mouth, so they all look a little surprised. Q says the tray of ginger doves I'm about to put in the oven may actually be ducks, so I quickly pinch each bill into a sharp beak. *They may have been ducks once, but they're doves now,* I tell him, and into the oven they go.

I have maybe three dozen spritz cookies in one box, three dozen ginger cutout cookies in another and dough for another four dozen in the icebox. I have two dozen walnut cookies in my white casserole dish. That's a lot of cookies, and I am not finished: I haven't made the rum balls yet, and they need to ripen a bit, so I'd better get on the ball with them. I'm not sure why I'm making all these cookies—nobody in the family is coming here for Christmas. For the first time since the girls left home years ago, they're not coming back for Christmas. We're all going to Corinna's house instead. Makes sense.

You don't think it means they never liked coming home, do you? I ask Q while he cooks dinner and I cut out ginger ducks and pinch their bills to turn them into doves. *No, it doesn't mean that at all,* he says. *It means they like having their own homes. They like being adults.*

I don't want to *be* Christmas to my kids. I don't want my death to suck all the joy out of it for them, don't want its delight to depart with me when I leave. I don't want this house, much as I love it, to be essential to them. I want them to be able to carry home with them in their hearts, wherever they go. I want the memories of us here to be more than the consciousness of loss. For as long as my mother lived, I returned home for Christmas. Packed the kids and all the presents and all the cookies I had made and made the trip—past the Quaker cemetery, past the frozen pond, past the stone gateposts that led to Eileen's farm, past the Grange Hall, past the filling station and the Nativity scene and the Christmas tree on the tiny village green, past my old school and the Methodist church and into their drive. I could no more imagine not being with her at Christmas than I could imagine not being myself. I could not imagine life without her.

She died just a month before my ordination, and soon it was Advent. I had other Christmas duties to attend to now, in my first parish, to help me ignore how much I missed her. And children who missed their Grandma to make Christmas for, now. Got it all done, somehow. Made all the cookies. Got the tree up. Managed it all fine, didn't even notice my broken heart. And I came to enjoy being the *doyenne* of it all, as the years passed.

But I am suddenly not that, anymore. I am not essential to it. They can have Christmas on their own, plan it and let me know how we fit in. This is jarring. But at least I didn't have to wait until I died to relinquish my Christmas throne.

Christmas

CHRISTMAS DAY

Pss 2, 85 * 110:1–5 (6–7), 132
Micah 4:1–5, 5:2–4
1 John 4:7–16
John 3:31–36

*. . . they shall beat their swords into plowshares, and their
spears into pruning hooks; nation shall not lift up sword against
nation, neither shall they learn war any more.*

MICAH 4:3

Which of the afflictions of humankind breaks your heart the most? In this passage, it's war: the suffering humanity chooses to inflict upon itself. Maybe the horror of war was fresh in Micah's mind—maybe Israel was in the midst of one when it was written.

But I write this as the terrible news continues to unfold about the tsunami in Southeast Asia. It gets worse with every new report. The worst natural disaster the world has ever known, perhaps; at least, it is the worst in human history. A natural disaster, nobody's fault. Just the earth, buckling and moving far beneath the sea.

Then there is famine. And illness—the plague of AIDS orphans hundreds of children in Africa and Asia every day, with no end in sight. And poverty. And prejudice. So many sorrows afflict us on this old earth.

But there must be a basic hope implanted in human beings by God: As hard as life can be, humanity never stops hoping. Hardly anybody wants to leave this world—most of us want to stay as long as we can. Israel's hope for a Messiah was decidedly this-worldly—that was the main reason they didn't recognize Jesus as the messiah: His kingdom was not of this world. We don't want to wait for another world. We want the transformation of *this* one.

And somehow both happen in Christ. He moves among the sick and the scorned of the earth, raising them out of their misery here and now—as a sign of a kingdom that is coming but also here, now, in its very beginnings: another way of being utterly unlike this one. *Take heart. I am with you. You fight and kill, sicken and die now—but it will not always be so.*

DECEMBER 26,
FEAST OF ST. STEPHEN

Pss 28, 30 * 118
2 Chronicles 24:17–22 * Wisdom 4:7–15
Acts 6:1–7 * Acts 7:59–8:8

"Lord, do not hold this sin against them. . . ."
ACTS 7:60

Right after the Feast of the Baby, while we're still wearing our soft smiles: the first martyr. *Lord, do not hold this sin against them,* Stephen cries, and then he dies. Just like Jesus, with words of forgiveness on his lips.

Interesting, then, that we usually understand the martyrdom of others in terms of our own guilt, as if the Church were critical of us for not being martyrs ourselves. And that we don't like martyrs— they make us feel guilty. And when we *are* acting like martyrs ourselves, on a bad day, involving ourselves in hated tasks with conspicuous and noisy dislike, but refusing to allow anyone to help us or to make it better in any way: We sure are ugly when we do that. Forgiveness is the farthest thing from our minds, and our behavior never makes other people value our contribution to their lives, as we hope it will. It just makes them feel guilty.

Stephen's approach to his own death is completely different. He embraces his own death as a gift. It's hard for us to hear of him, or any joyful martyr, without thinking of the suicide bombers of our own age—they're happy, too. Maybe they're all sick: Stephen, the suicide bombers. Maybe even Jesus.

But there are some important differences between Jesus, or Stephen, and a suicide bomber. The first is, of course, that neither

Jesus nor Stephen takes other people with them, while the suicide bomber's purpose is to kill as many people as he can, and he's willing to die to do it.

But equally important is the forgiveness part: Both Jesus and Stephen ask God's forgiveness on their tormentors. No suicide bomber ever does that. His sacrifice is in the service of hate. The gift of a true martyr is all about love.

DECEMBER 27, FEAST OF ST. JOHN

Pss 97, 98 * 145
Proverbs 8:22–30 * Isaiah 44:1–8
John 13:20–35
1 John 5:1–12

"Very truly, I tell you, whoever receives one whom I send receives me; and whoever receives me receives him who sent me."

JOHN 13:20

The visit was always the same: I would drive to the Fergusons' little house and there they would be, waiting for me in their tiny living room. Madeleine's mother was still alive then, and we would have communion together. She couldn't see very well, and I was never too sure she understood what we were doing with the little cup and plate, but she always received it politely and smiled a faraway smile.

Then Mrs. Gerrecht became still more frail, and had to be in the hospital. So I would drive to the little house and George would get out his big car—a Cadillac? I forget, but it was about the size of their house—and he would drive us all to give her communion in the hospital. Then we would come home, and they would set out cookies and tea—always the same cookies, cookies from Denmark, in a round blue tin box, and we would chat about things I don't even remember now. Nothing theological. Nothing much, really.

And then I would get in my car and drive back to the church to enter the visit into the book: Day: *Feast of St. John*. Place: *Ferguson home* Number present: *Four*. Until Madeleine's mother finally died, and then the home visits stopped except when Madeleine herself became ill, which was frequent. Then there were three. Both Fergusons have been gone for some years now. I don't know how many times I visited them over the years. I don't know that we ever talked about anything of great magnitude, and we certainly didn't *do* anything of note: just had communion and cookies and tea afterward. Bread, wine, cookies, and tea. So ordinary.

We think that big things are liable to happen when God sends somebody somewhere. But I think the things that happen then are usually pretty small. The kingdom of God is built of small things, too, not just of amazing big ones.

DECEMBER 28,
FEAST OF THE HOLY INNOCENTS

Pss 2, 26 * 19, 126
Isaiah 49:13–23 * Isaiah 54:1–13
Matthew 18:1–14 * Mark 10:13–16

He called a child, whom he put among them.
MATTHEW 18:2

So many children lost in the Indian Ocean tsunami. And what about the ones who survive: What is it like to be twelve years old and to have lost your whole family?

Children seem to get the worst of just about every large disaster, and the loss of them hurts us more than the loss of adults. Why is that? We call the children murdered by wicked Herod "The Holy Innocents," but we know that many adults are killed and injured through no fault of their own, too.

I guess we know that adults usually have a head start. We're experienced, and more likely to get ourselves out of a dangerous situation.

Sometimes it doesn't work, of course—the tsunami took no notice of anybody's age—but we have more to work with than little ones have.

And also: We don't quite feel *innocent*, like they are. We've lived life, and learned what we could learn in the time we've had thus far. We've done rather well at parts of it and should have done better in others—we know which ones those are. Most of us want to live a lot longer, but all of us have had at least a taste.

They didn't even get a *taste*. That's what offends us. Maybe they would have been good people and maybe they would have been bad. Probably they would have been like us, a little of both. But at least they deserved a taste of the feast the world offers us every day.

CHRISTMAS I

Pss 93, 96 * 34
1 Samuel 1:1–2, 7b–28
Colossians 1:9–20
Luke 2:22–40

"How long will you make a drunken spectacle of yourself?
Put away your wine."
1 SAMUEL 1:14

Eli thought Hannah was drunk. She answers him matter-of-factly, and we are not told if she was angry at being so misunderstood.

I wonder if women alcoholics labored then under the same burden of shame and secrecy that binds them today? Probably. Ask a woman in recovery about the day she admitted to herself that her drinking had gotten beyond her control—better yet, ask her about the days and weeks and years before that, about how she explained herself to herself, about how angry it made her when anyone in her family brought it up. Ask her about hiding the evidence in the kitchen trash can, way down deep. Ask her about sitting up after everyone had gone to bed, about her silent husband when she finally got there herself, about how she knew he was awake and wanting to talk to her about it and how she pretended she thought he was asleep, night after night. Ask her about the lovely meals she prepared, and how she congratulated herself on each one of them: See, this meal is evidence that I'm okay, that there's nothing wrong. Here, taste this!

Boys will be boys, of course. Boys are wild. You never know what a boy will do. But girls are ladies. Girls behave themselves. Girls are good. Good girls aren't alcoholics. I don't know a single woman in recovery who did not wrestle with the issue of her goodness in a way different from the way men do.

In sobriety, they see their goodness again. It was never gone. They weren't misbehaving on purpose: They were in the grip of something bigger than they were, and now they have gotten free. None of the things they tried to do to make up for their drinking made up for it, but every good thing they were before, they still are. And many other good things besides.

But when they go to a meeting, they don't arrive with the lists of accomplishments they might have made before they got sober. They just slide into their seats. When it's their turn to speak, they just say, *Hi, I'm M——, and I'm an alcoholic.*

DECEMBER 29

Pss 18:1–20 * 18:21–50
2 Samuel 23:13–17b
2 John 1–13
John 2:1–11

But he would not drink of it; he poured it out to the Lord.
2 SAMUEL 23:16

And after all that, David won't drink. I bet the three warriors had all they could do not to strangle him then and there.

I remember reading about a crush Frank Sinatra had on Ava Gardner—he carried his torch a little longer than she carried hers, and soon she flew off to Rome without him. Knowing she loved angel food cake, he prevailed on his friend Lauren Bacall to carry an angel food cake on her lap all the way from New York to Rome. That was a long flight in those days. When Ava received the cake, she didn't even open it—just rolled her eyes and set it down on her dressing table. She was over angel food and over Frank, I guess; Lauren didn't say anything, but I think Ava was lucky to have survived.

When someone does you a conspicuous favor, you must accept it graciously. If someone risks his life to get you a drink, drink, for heaven's sake. Such large acts in the provision of such small pleasures are strong signs of affection, no? They should be met with equal devotion, right?

But wait—there is a certain discomfort in being on the receiving end of such devotion. One knows one's own tiniest wish does not outweigh another's safety or comfort. We don't really want a slave. We want a partner. An equal.

So don't bring me an angel food cake at great effort and expense, and especially don't drag a mutual friend into your neediness. Be a peer: Respect me enough to argue with me, say, if you catch me behaving in a manner unworthy of myself. Now that's an honor.

DECEMBER 30

Pss 20, 21:1–7 (8–14) * 23, 27
1 Kings 17:17–24
John 4:46–54
3 John 1–15

*"Beloved, do not imitate what is evil, but imitate
what is good. Whoever does good is from God;
whoever does evil has not seen God."*
3 JOHN 11

Pen and ink seemed too distant to this writer: He wanted the direct intimacy of a visit. We do not know if he ever got it, as this is the last of the letters of John we have.

I wonder what he would have thought of e-mail. Now a pen-and-ink letter is a rare intimacy: mostly, we just press "send." E-mail has made some of us verbose communicators, while others of us have become much more terse, shooting off a succinct "lol" or "idk"* into the ether. Most everyone sees the same thing: You get five or six copies of the same joke or inspirational poem, complete with the immense pedigree of the other people who have received and forwarded it before it came to you, phalanxes of single-space screen names, all crowded together as you scroll down looking for whatever it was you were sent.

Would we go back to a simpler time, if we could? Back to a time when a letter took months or even years to reach its recipient? Back to a time when it was not at all unusual for the sender to have died in the interval between his composition of the letter and your receiving it? News traveled so slowly then. Today, it is lightning.

But even now, there is no substitute for face-to-face. People who become e-mail buddies—and I have known several who met their spouses in this way—still long to meet in person. And worry about the meeting: *Will I disappoint in the flesh? Will he like me as much as he likes me online? And will I like him?*

The self I present is real enough, but it is not the whole of who I am. Meet me in person and you see a thousand things of which I might be totally unaware: these are also me. We are complicated. It takes some time and some slow attention to read the book of us.

---

* "idk" means "I don't know; "lol" means "laugh out loud." But you knew that.

DECEMBER 31,
EVE OF HOLY NAME

Pss 46, 48 * 90
1 Kings 3:5–14 * Isaiah 65:15b–25
James 4:13–17; 5:7–11 * Revelation 21:1–6
John 5:1–15

"Sir, I have no one to put me into the pool when the water is stirred up; and while I am making my way, someone else steps down ahead of me."

JOHN 5:7

This was a magic pool: In a verse not present in every translation of this passage, we learn that an angel sometimes came to the pool and "troubled the water," that is, made it churn. It was magic when that happened: first one in was guaranteed a healing.

But there was a hierarchy of privilege among the infirm, as there is among the well: The weakest among them could not hope to be first, not ever. The stronger ones always got there first. This paralyzed man always lagged behind. For years the waters had offered him hope, but he was too ill to grasp it. A bitter discouragement must have crept into his heart whenever he saw the waters begin to tremble: Here we go again.

So it is to him that Jesus turns. To the one in greatest need, to the weakest. It is to the sick that the doctor comes, Jesus says in another place, not to the well. Of course it is. It's the sick who need a doctor.

Sometimes it is the world that shuts us out of the healing pool: The poor get sick more often than the wealthy, and they get sicker. And sometimes it is our own paralysis: We've been stuck in our weakness for so long, we can't even imagine being free. It has become part of our identity to be weak.

Besides healing itself, Jesus shows us the way to prepare for healing. Sometimes he heals people in stages. Sometimes he explores the spiritual backdrop to their physical ailments. Sometimes, afterwards, he invites them to confront the healing power of God and what it has meant to have received it. His healings are rarely simple acts: They all have meanings beyond the restoration of physical health. They are not just about the body: They are about spirit, and world, and even about justice. There's an ecology to the healings of Jesus. Everything is connected to everything else.

FEAST OF THE HOLY NAME

Pss 103 * 148
Isaiah 62:1–5, 10–12
Revelation 19:11–16
Matthew 1:18–25

Her husband Joseph, being a righteous man
and unwilling to expose her to public disgrace,
planned to dismiss her quietly.
MATTHEW 1:19

What might public shaming have done to Mary, the mother of our Lord? It might have killed her: The law permitted a woman caught in such a position to be stoned to death. But Joseph was a just man, Matthew says. And he may already have loved the woman who was to be his wife. He didn't want to hurt her. And he didn't know any other way to handle this situation—although God was about to show him another way.

Shame kills people today, too. The enormous number of people who suffer and die from AIDS in Africa has not wiped out the stigma attached to the disease in many places: Some people still prefer to suffer and die alone, rather than expose their families to the shame of their diagnosis.

But American visitors to the AIDS clinics in southern Africa frequently remark upon the dignity of the patients there, and upon the quiet, stubborn love of their families, who journey miles with them to the treatment centers, bringing food and bedding from home. Familial love—family understood much more broadly than we understand it here, including dozens, perhaps scores of related people—is a source of spiritual power in Africa, undergirding situations that might otherwise be unbearable. Faced with intractable suffering, love conquers in the end, simply by refusing to turn away.

How did AIDS come into a family's life? Was the mother's first hint of her husband's infidelity her own infection, a baby's first experience of HIV/AIDS in the womb? Or was it the sad facts of family life in many villages: the long absence of the father in a work camp, where loneliness and a little cash buys brief comfort and then endless suffering, and the act of love brings it all tragically home?

We might think that the means of transmission would make a big difference in the degree of shame a family experiences, but a visit to such a clinic tells us that it need not be so. It doesn't matter how you got it: You are a human being until the very end, a life worth prolonging as long as it is possible, a life worth mourning when it is finished. The children of the dead and dying shock visitors with their joy: They are children of tragedy, yes, but they are still children, one American visitor says, and she tells of how they blew bubbles together. And how the children laughed and laughed.

How did Mary become pregnant, people in her town must have asked. There must have been a stigma attached to her, too. But, however it happened, it mattered less in the end than who the child *was* who would be born. At the foot of the cross, her unusual pregnancy didn't set her apart from any other bereaved mother: What kept her there was stubborn love, the same love that binds together the families of the stricken all over the world.

CHRISTMAS II

Pss 66, 67 * 145
Wisdom 7:3–14
Colossians 3:12–17
John 6:41–47

. . . there is for all one entrance into life,
and one way out.
WISDOM 7:6

Perhaps we don't all arrive with equal potential, but we all arrive with some. And we look alike in our hospital basinets—new parents look at the nametags, just to be sure they have the right little screamer, that we are who they think we are. Our personalities, present from the beginning in rudimentary form, must develop. We become who we will be, but we are not our adult selves at first. The beginning of life doesn't vary much.

Neither does the end. Every death bed is familiar: As the strong spirit becomes more intent on the next world, what remains in this one grows more and more simple: breath, heartbeat, sleep. Less and less to do as less is possible. Our true selves are already somewhere else.

Between the beginning and the end, though, we vary considerably: brilliant and dull, beautiful and plain, rich and poor. All of our energy goes into creating these variations, into trying to move from one to another. We want to get ahead. We are programmed to grow and to desire growth: We suffer when either the growth or our desire for it is impeded.

It is a fact of life on earth that poverty impedes both growth and, eventually desire for growth. It grinds hope down to the very nub, and it becomes no longer possible even to imagine a better world, a more active self. The amputation of a limb is not sadder than this cruel sucking away of hope.

JANUARY 2

Pss 34 * 33
1 Kings 19:1–8
Ephesians 4:1–16
John 6:1–14

*But speaking the truth in love, we must grow up
in every way into him who is the head. . . .*
EPHESIANS 4:15

Does this make me look fat? So, how was my sermon? Did you enjoy your dinner?

What to say? It's important to tell the truth, and the truth is going to hurt. Almost always people tell the kind lie about these things. Is there a way to be honest and kind?

Probably we don't think enough about the timing of our truth. When she's staring into the mirror and has nothing else to wear to an event that's fifteen minutes from now isn't the time for candor. *You look wonderful!* will have to do for now. But there will come another time, a calmer time, a time not so rushed and not quite so vulnerable, when you can bring it up. *You know, you did look good at the party the other night, but I was thinking today that a V-neckline might be a better choice and was wondering if we could go and try some on sometime, so you can see what I mean. Want to?*

In grading an essay, you must find *something* to compliment, and you must begin your evaluation with it, even if it can only be *I just love your font!* And then you can move on to the harder stuff, which is what you owe someone who has asked you to help her become a better writer. But you do need to find that kind word, and find it first, so that she will be able to hear what she really needs to know.

Speak the truth in love, and find the right time and the right way to speak it. It's true that lies aren't loving, but a quick truth offered with no thought for how it might land might not be, either.

JANUARY 3

Pss 68 * 72
1 Kings 19:9–18
Ephesians 4:17–32
John 6:15–27

Thieves must give up stealing; rather let them labor
and work honestly with their own hands. . . .
EPHESIANS 4:28

Our attitudes toward incarceration are seasonal. Recently, the trend has been toward harshness: Lock 'em up, throw away the key, no frills. Don't even let them have an AA meeting. And then, later, throw up our hands and wonder why they return to the life they left when they came inside.

Why do you sell drugs? Why don't you get a job? *Because I don't know how to do anything else. I never finished high school. I got a monkey on my back myself—I couldn't go without the stuff for more than a couple of hours.*

And when there are services directed toward helping inmates get their lives together, the public reacts negatively: outside, people think prison is easy. *You don't have to work. You live and sleep for nothing. Heck, I had to work* my *way through school. These guys get college courses for free.*

Some of them won't turn around, no matter how many degrees they get in prison. Some of them won't get better. But some will. Some might. Some can. We owe it to ourselves, mostly, to allow as many as can to break free from the moral prison that holds them as tightly as any prison bars.

And those who can't? Won't? Never will? We owe it to ourselves and to them to find ways to make them useful to society. Everyone needs to be productive in some way, and society needs it from everyone. In productivity we mirror the creativity of God. Everyone needs to do that, in whatever way is possible, or nothing else will ever be possible. True for everyone. And that includes incarcerated people.

JANUARY 4

Pss 85, 87 * 89:1–29
Joshua 3:14–4:7
Ephesians 5:1–20
John 9:1–12, 35–38

"Then I went and washed and received my sight."
JOHN 9:11

What is missing, in the long story of the blind man's healing and the subsequent hubbub among the authorities, is the laughter from the crowd that heard the story for the first time. Because they must have *howled*: Here is Jesus giving a blind man sight, God acting mightily to interrupt a human sorrow and give us a foretaste of the end of all sorrow, and right away the power people zero in on whether he had the right to do it, whether the man was really the blind man they remembered or a sighted look-alike, whether the healing was a fake, whether the man was good or bad, whether his *mom and dad* were good or bad, for heaven's sake. The story got better and better with each objection.

The blind man must have been accustomed to the uninvited touch of strangers. He could never see people coming toward him— someone touched him and he couldn't see who it was. Probably he had been the victim of crime, sometimes—the disabled are easy marks for thieves. Someone he doesn't know rubs mud in his eyes and tells him to go and wash, and he stumbles off. Best not to argue, he had learned long ago. Best to do what you're told. You never know what might happen.

So we hear no protest from the blind man, no indignant *Hey! Whaddaya think you're doin'?* when Jesus performs his eccentric healing. He is silent and he obeys, turns and makes his halting way down to the water and does as he is told. He tells the tale in just that matter-of-fact way, as if it were normal. Other people are excited, but the formerly blind man remains calm, quietly exasperated by all the noise. And when everyone is finished with him, too distressed by his miracle to want anything more to do with him, he continues his quiet exploration of the miracle. He is accustomed to his own isolation: People have left him alone all his life. He has had a lot of time to think, and he is used to solitary thinking. And now he goes in search of this man who healed him. To find out what it will mean to see.

JANUARY 5, EVE OF EPIPHANY

Pss 2, 110:1–5 (6–7)
Jonah 2:2–9
Ephesians 6:10–20
John 11:17–27, 38–44

. . . I am an ambassador in chains. . . .
EPHESIANS 6:20

A physical prison isn't always a spiritual one. Nelson Mandela was a prisoner on Robben Island for twenty-seven years, and his moral authority grew with every year that passed. Much can be taken from us—physical freedom and physical health, fellowship with those we love. But the freedom of the mind and spirit is ours to keep. We are in charge of it.

Not that it is unaffected by what is done to us. You have to fight for your own spirit sometimes: It is strong, but it is not invulnerable. Sometimes it needs a defender.

The best defense for a spirit under attack is prayer. How do you pray for the protection of your own spirit? Don't worry if you are too broken to find the words: Words aren't as necessary in prayer as we imagine them to be, for God knows what's going on already. All we really have to do is lift our broken spirits to God, like a child handing a broken toy to her mother or father; *Here*, she whimpers, *fix this.* We don't even have to know what's really wrong; God already knows. We just have to hand it over. *Here. Fix this.*

Like Nelson Mandela, Paul was able to serve even in prison. We are able to serve, even when we are still broken, even while God is still fixing us. God specializes in making a great deal out of not very much. Unexpected protection and unexpected power. Unexpected healing. Unexpected repair. After a while, we learn to expect it.

Epiphany

FEAST OF THE EPIPHANY

Pss 46, 97 * 96, 100
Isaiah 49:1–7
Revelation 21:22–27
Matthew 12:14–21

"And in his name the Gentiles will hope."
MATTHEW 12:21

Gentiles? By the time Matthew is writing, it ruffles no feathers to say such a thing: that faith in Christ is for the Gentiles as well. For everyone. By the time Matthew writes, the battles between St. Paul and the Judaizers in Jerusalem are over, and we know that a Greek or African convert to Christianity doesn't have to become a Jew first, on his way to being baptized. We already know that Christianity is not going to be just a peculiar sect of Judaism—although Matthew writes from within a Jewish context. It will be much wider than just the people of Israel.

And we are beginning to realize that the length of days until the return of Christ at the end of time could be—will be—*long*. By the time Matthew writes, we want to know how to live life, how to relate to the power of the state and to society, how to relate the stories of Jesus to ages far distant from him. Maybe even as far as our own age. Maybe even beyond.

Christ is for everyone. He is not our own invention, and we cannot invent him to look like us or sound like us or think like us. He will not conveniently mirror our prejudices or baptize our parochialism. He encompasses the changes of human history, sees them all and lives in them all—the project of finding a golden age in the past and claiming it as exclusively his, excluding all other ages, is a whistling into the wind.

JANUARY 7

Psalm 103 * 114, 115
Deuteronomy 8:1–3
Colossians 1:1–14
John 6:30–33, 48, 51

"What sign are you going to give us then,
so that we may see it and believe you?"
JOHN 6:30

The adult son of friends had a seizure the other night, and before anyone knew which end was up, he was in surgery for a rapacious brain tumor. No clue that such a thing had been growing inside him. It is fast-growing and very dangerous. The mother wrote of her anger at its "invasion of the sacred precincts of my son's brain." It was as if it were a predatory animal. Or a demon.

Now, slowly—but more quickly than any of us expected, he is on the mend. As much of the tumor as could be removed safely was excised, and chemotherapy in the form of flat discs was placed on what remained of the growth. They looked like communion wafers, she wrote. The danger of swelling has receded, and he has begun to regain some of his faculties.

And so their prayers have been answered with healing, mediated by the miracle of modern medicine. They are exhausted and grateful. Their son, awakening to the reality of what has occurred in this short span of time, laughs and weeps by turn as he comes to grips with his terrible wounding, his jarring deliverance, his wait for a final word, his uncertain future: It is hard to face having been young and strong and then suddenly, being only young.

Is that the sign of Christ's presence? That he is healing and his prognosis improves every day? And might someone else look at the same circumstance and see only sorrow: a young man, stricken ill, perhaps mortally so, through no fault of his own, in pain and frightened? Is he healing? Well, why was he stricken in the first place?

This is how we know the limitation of signs when it comes to encountering Christ. They mean different things to different people.

Signs are part of history, and history changes, plunges us into despair and back out again, sometimes just leaves us there. We can't gauge the presence of God using history as a barometer: History doesn't measure God. It is God who measures history.

JANUARY 8

Pss 117, 118 * 112, 113
Exodus 17:1–7
Colossians 1:15–23
John 7:37–52

From the wilderness of Sin the whole congregation
of the Israelites journeyed by stages. . . .
EXODUS 17:1

No, it's not a pun or an allegory—this time, "Sin" is a real place name. It's only a word for "moral failure" in English. It didn't mean that in the Egyptian language.

But it's just too good a line to let go, and people have violated the integrity of biblical texts in the service of much less worthy causes: We do depart from sin by stages, most of the time. We make any number of false endings before we finally wriggle free.

Was my cigarette smoking sinful? I certainly didn't think so at the time. It seemed an entirely private matter to me. It seemed like a matter of my own civil rights, in fact: Who was anybody else to tell me what to do? Didn't I have the right to smoke, even if it *was* bad for me? Wasn't it my life?

Yes, it was. But my children needed me. And the example of my smoking would encourage them to do so—surely my civil rights didn't extend to encouraging children to do themselves harm. And I exhaled death with every breath: We shared the air in our house, and I polluted it daily.

I tried and tried to stop, before I finally did. Failed many times. God led the Israelites with fire by night and cloud by day, led them constantly. But they didn't follow very constantly—there were many failures along the way. They could only make the journey from the wilderness of Sin the way I made it, the way we all make it: one step at a time.

JANUARY 9

Pss 121, 122, 123 * 131, 132
Isaiah 45:14–19
Colossians 1:24–2:7
John 8:12–19

"You are testifying in your own behalf;
your testimony is not valid."

JOHN 8:13

By now, you know your strengths and your weaknesses. You can answer an interviewer who wants you to spell them out, and you know better than to pad your resume: If you claim a competence you do not possess, they're going to know.

They do want to hear from you about you, but they are also interested in your references. This is harder than it used to be; most human resources people refuse to elaborate on your tenure with them: *Yes, he worked here from such-and-such a date to such-and-such a date.* Period.

Perhaps you'll get a subtle non-answer to a direct question: *I understand there's a law against saying something bad about someone in these circumstances,* one HR person I know says when the news is really not good, *so perhaps you ought to contact somebody else.* Whew. That would do it for me.

Testimony is supposed to be disinterested. That's why our own self-evaluation isn't enough: We are not neutral about ourselves. We want the job. But, of course, nobody is neutral about anything—no human resources manager, no interviewer, no witness. Certainly no lawyer. Everyone has biases, conscious ones or unconscious ones.

In the end, witnesses can only be so reliable. In the end, we still have to weigh what they say, no matter who they are. In the end, we will not be spared having to render a judgment ourselves, about everything.

Who is Jesus, really? What will happen if I follow him? What's the truth? What can you tell me to assure me that what I am about to do will work out well? We can tell each other a fair amount about ourselves, about somebody else, and also about Christ. But in the end, we each must choose for ourselves.

JANUARY 10

Pss 138, 139:1–17 (18–23) * 147
Jeremiah 23:1–8
Colossians 2:8–23
John 10:7–17

*. . . God made you alive together with him,
when he forgave us all our trespasses, erasing
the record that stood against us with its legal demands.
He set this aside, nailing it to the cross.*
COLOSSIANS 2:13–14

This is the theology of the Atonement. It's not as popular in some circles these days as it used to be—there are people who don't want to think much about our having any sins, and so it would be difficult for them to be very excited about the prospect of having our sins forgiven.

But dammit, we *do* have sins. We always have had them. We have lots of them. On my very best day, I have tons. Large and small—mostly small, but sometimes serious ways in which I have hurt someone, usually someone I love very much.

Why don't we want to own up to this? It must be because we think we disqualify ourselves for the love of God by admitting to wrongdoing. We must think God is like us, stingy in love, edgy, careful, keeping score. But the reverse is true, and that's the whole point of the Atonement. God is profligate in his love. It is the sinners to whom Christ wishes to speak first. We are the ones he chooses. We are the ones who need him—only sick people need the physician. He has little with which to occupy his time among the well.

That we have sins from which we regularly need deliverance in no way obscures the image of God in each of us. Again, that's the whole point: We deserve better than to put ourselves and others through hell at times, but we can't seem to stop doing it under our own power. We need a savior.

I remember how annoyed my children were at being small. Hated being powerless. I hate it, too. But it has been only in getting clear about my weaknesses that I have found whatever strength I've found in life. It has worked every time. Regularly. Because God is regularly very good, no matter what might or might not be happening with me on a given day.

JANUARY 11

Pss 148, 150 * 91, 92
Isaiah 55:3–9
Colossians 3:1–17
John 14:6–14

In that renewal there is no longer Greek and Jew,
circumcised and uncircumcised, barbarian, Scythian,
slave and free; but Christ is all and in all!
COLOSSIANS 3:11

You know that people have used scripture to justify slavery. And to justify denying the dignity of women. You know that people have used scripture to argue against the dignity of gay and lesbian people. You may know that people used scripture to defend the horrors of the Holocaust and of the Inquisition. *It's right there in the book,* someone will say, pointing to a passage in Romans or Leviticus.

But the Bible is not a book. It's a *group* of books. It was written over a period of at least a thousand years, from beginning to end, and it was written in several different languages by people of several different cultures and eras. They all reflected their cultures in the way they wrote.

When Paul wrote these words, he was thinking outside the box of his own culture and training. He was arguing for something his fellow Jews would say was definitely *not* in the book. It must certainly have been hard for him to do this: Everyone he had valued his whole life long was certain not to understand what he was doing and to disapprove utterly. Friends must have become enemies overnight. It cost him to write this, and he cannot have done it lightly.

As it costs us to live it, centuries later. The world does not reward inclusivity: It laughs at it. You don't get the brass ring if you don't play the world's game. To the world, you look foolish. You have low standards. Low morals, even. You have no respect for tradition. You are—a favorite dismissive church term of late—*trendy*.

Well, you can't please everyone. But if it's *trendy* to do in my era what Paul did in his, two thousand years ago, I'll take it.

JANUARY 12,
EVE OF EPIPHANY I

Pss 98, 99, (100) * 104
Genesis 49:1–2, 8–12 * Isaiah 61:1–9
Colossians 3:18–4:6 * Galatians 3:23–29, 4:4–7
John 15:1–16

Wives, be subject to your husbands, as is fitting in the Lord.
COLOSSIANS 3:18

So here we are, then: In literally his next breath, Paul seems to undo much of the radicalism of what we read yesterday. This is what drives people crazy about Paul: He starts off so well, and then he seems to cave in to old prejudices.

Most people who study this letter with that difficulty in mind find some explanation in the early Church's belief that the end of the world was coming toward them like a runaway train. Very soon, they thought, Jesus would return on clouds of glory and wind things up here. Don't worry if your life is hard—it's almost over. And so what we would call "social justice" is not large in their day-to-day life: They think they're about to go to heaven, and everything will be worked out there. There won't *be* any society.

And you? What would you do if you thought the world was ending tomorrow? Who would you call? Where would you have dinner? Would you take up smoking again? Sometimes a group of people in recovery talks about that over coffee after a meeting: Would I drink again if I knew I were going to die tomorrow? Much laughter and joking ensues when someone poses this hypothetical situation. *But really*, someone says at last, *what would you do?* And mostly the answer is the same: I would go to a meeting. I wouldn't drink. I'd work the program that brought me back from the dead the first time.

Probably we'd keep doing the things that bring us closer to God during our lives, if we thought we were going to be with God tomorrow. We'd be thinking of the future, not of the past. It would be almost upon us, and we would be all about getting ready.

SUNDAY, EPIPHANY I

Pss 146, 147 * 111, 112, 113
Genesis 1:1–2:3
Ephesians 1:3–14
John 1:29–34

. . . and he rested on the seventh day from all the work that he had done. So God blessed the seventh day, and hallowed it. . . .
GENESIS 2:2–3

Ah. The last service of the morning—wherever I am on Sunday, it's a good feeling. Perhaps I have lunch with someone from the church, or perhaps I just get back on the road. If it is the former, everyone is feeling the same way, and we are relaxed and funny as we eat. *Ah.*

And if it is the latter? Usually I am driving home. Then it's Jonathan Schwartz—he starts playing music at noon here in New York and finishes at 4 p.m., four wonderful hours of wonderful songs by performers everyone loves, and nobody to whom I must talk. The miles back home unfold, passing scenery I passed this morning while it was still too dark to see it properly, and I am there before I know it.

Then a nap. The paper. More music on the radio. Maybe a nice bubble bath, toward evening—my day has ended, but I know that the clergy I left back at the parish I visited today probably have another service in the evening, hospital calls to make. Some even have vestry meetings on Sunday afternoons, a terrible thing to do to the Lord's Day, if you ask me.

Most people who make church happen for others must make another day our Sabbath. An untouchable day—you can go for many days, working every day, and not realize how weary you are. How much you need the healing a day of rest brings. You become a little like a hamster on his squeaky wheel: just can't stop running. Just keep running, going exactly nowhere. It's a dark time of year, this season of light. The days are short, and the weather here is cold. It is easy to keep your eyes on the ground and never look up, just trudge on and on. Easy, perhaps, but not very holy, and not God's will for his exhausted servants. Stop. Pull back. Take the day. It will all still be here the next morning.

MONDAY IN EPIPHANY I

Pss 1, 2, 3 * 4, 7
Genesis 2:4–9 (10–15) 16–25
Hebrews 1:1–14
John 1:1–18

Long ago God spoke to our ancestors in many
and various ways by the prophets, but in these last days
he has spoken to us by a Son. . . .
HEBREWS 1:1–2

Some of the prophets were strange birds. Jeremiah walked around his city naked, wearing a heavy wooden yoke—the people of Israel would become slaves, he was saying. Ezekiel saw things other people didn't see, including what some people are sure must have been a flying saucer, and he saw a valley of dry bones come back to life. Amos saw things, too, visions of common objects: a basket of summer fruit, a carpenter's level, and drew conclusions from these things about the deplorable moral state of his countrymen. A couple of the prophets allegorized their love lives: Their sexual relationships with the women in their lives were models of God's relationship with the people of Israel, and they named the children resulting from these unions allegorically: If you don't like your given name, just be thankful you're not Hosea's daughter. Her name was "Not-My-People." And her little brother? "Not Pitied."

So their messages weren't always models of clarity and common sense. They were dramatic and poetic, not literal. They were the performance artists of their day. Over the top.

I would rather speak to God through the more intelligible means of Jesus. Jesus is like us and knows us, and because he is the Christ, the Son of but also the actual enfleshing of the unknowable God who knows us so well, he can understand us. When he comes to us, God has come to us. Not a messenger. God himself.

How do we begin to speak to God? We begin by listening—let yourself grow quiet. Don't worry about distractions, everybody has 'em, and they'll go away if you just sit there patiently and wait them out. And then tell Jesus you're not sure how to proceed, that you've never been very good at this, that you sometimes question your own sincerity. Tell him all these things he already knows. And then listen some more: Some of what comes into your mind will be the voice of Christ speaking directly to you in the language of your own mind and spirit.

TUESDAY IN EPIPHANY I

Pss 5, 6 * 10, 11
Genesis 3:1–24
Hebrews 2:1–10
John 1:19–28

*Now the serpent was more crafty than any other
wild animal that the Lord God had made.*

GENESIS 3:1

Actually, they're not all that smart, snakes. They're just quiet and mysterious-looking. They don't have a wide repertoire of activities or reactions—you'll never teach a snake to fetch. Emotions seem foreign to them. In that and in many ways, they are quite different from us. That's why we don't like them.

And yet—there is a species of highly poisonous water snake native to the barrier reefs of Australia that has become accustomed to the underwater visits of human beings. They flock to the place where the divers come, sitting vertically in the water and watching the interlopers. They do not attack; that is not why they have come. They are just curious. They want to see what we're doing.

A serpent plays the villain in the tragedy of Adam and Eve—we are told, at the end of the tale, that his role in it is the reason all his descendents have to slither along on the ground. But it turns out that some of them swim. And some of them, apparently, go sightseeing.

Alone of all the animals, the snake repels us viscerally. Even non-poisonous, garden-helpful snakes repel us. It makes little sense—we cuddle our teddy bears, some of whose living cousins could kill us with one swipe of their terrible claws. We love bears. It's snakes we can't stand.

Interesting and odd on our part. And on the part of the writer of Genesis, as well: The snake is utterly impassive. Its face betrays no emotion. And yet its biblical task was tempting human emotions—curiosity, perversity, lust for power. Very odd indeed, because snakes don't seem to lust for anything. In Genesis, the snake works to lure us into a vortex of sin in which it would never share. To inaugurate the mayhem we can get ourselves into without ever participating in it itself. We are left permanently wounded, chronically unfree. And the snake just slides silently away.

WEDNESDAY IN EPIPHANY I

Pss 119:1–24 * 12, 13, 14
Genesis 4:1–16
Hebrews 2:11–18
John 1: (29–34) 35–42

One of the two who heard John speak and followed him was Andrew, Simon Peter's brother. He first found his brother Simon and said to him, "We have found the Messiah" (which is translated Anointed). He brought Simon to Jesus, who looked at him and said, "You are Simon, son of John. You are to be called Cephas" (which is translated Peter).

JOHN 1:40–42

My part was a small one—one scene. A handful of lines and actions—I was a nurse, engaged to care for the Elephant Man, and I couldn't handle either his appearance or his stench. That was about the extent of my role.

You know, said Lee Winston, after watching me do a mediocre job in my small part, *for a part like that, one in which you do one scene and the audience never sees you again, you're the star of that one scene. Its only purpose is for you to be there and tell the audience what it is you know—the playwright wouldn't have put your character in the play if that character didn't have something to say the audience needs to hear and that only she can say. So take the stage. It's only one scene, but it's not a small part.*

I never forgot what he told me. He was absolutely right, I saw immediately: only we can do what we do, and we are each the star of the scene we're in. Maybe we're not the star of the whole play—but our scene is our scene.

Andrew doesn't have what today would be called a high profile—he listens to a sermon and then goes and gets his brother to listen to the preacher. That's pretty much it for Andrew. But he knew, on the strength of that one encounter, that he had seen the Messiah, and he knew he had to share that knowledge. So it is all-but-anonymous Andrew, not his famous brother, who is the first evangelist.

It's important to be important, I guess. But not everyone is called to high visibility—in fact, hardly any of us are. Almost all of us work our way through life and faith considerably below the radar of public awareness. Not many people know about us.

But that doesn't mean we don't matter. Everyone who acts, on however modest a stage, affects others. We don't even know, until later on, who all those others are—a moment you forgot long ago may have changed the life of the person who was with you. Your unsung steadiness may be the thing for which you are lovingly remembered—it may have prompted someone to think for the first time that God, too, may be dependable.

THURSDAY IN EPIPHANY I

Pss 18:1–20 * 18:21–50
Genesis 4:17–26
Hebrews 3:1–11
John 1:43–51

Cain knew his wife, and she conceived
and bore Enoch; and he built a city,
and named it Enoch after his son Enoch.
GENESIS 4:17

Wait a minute—wife? What wife? Where did Cain get a wife? And who *lived* in that city? Where did all these people come from, if Cain's mom and dad were the first two people on earth?

The writer of this portion of Genesis isn't at all concerned about this making sense: We are the only literalists in this encounter. He was just writing a story about how human beings interact with God, imagining how we became the way we are. He never thought he was writing history.

It's odd to see so many modern Americans as angry as so many of them are by an approach to the book of Genesis other than a literal one. To see the earnestness with which they defend its dubious scientific possibility, as if salvation depended upon fundamentalism. I don't understand it.

On your way to sleep, sometimes, or while staring into a cracking fire, you wonder: How many pairs of eyes have stared into a fire just this way? How many are the generations? What was the past like? In a movie or a book, people travel through time and meet famous figures in human history: You stare into the fire and think of Adam and Eve, of a moment when the significance of our brain size and opposable digits teetered for a second and then tipped toward the path to poetry, literature, to the idea of God. Toward war and peace, cities, rocket ships. How long it has been since that first moment? How many stories have we dreamed about it?

But sometimes it seems not to have been long at all.

FRIDAY IN EPIPHANY I

Pss 16, 17 * 22
Genesis 6:1–8
Hebrews 3:12–19
John 2:1–12

The Nephilim were on the earth in those days—and also afterward—when the sons of God went in to the daughters of humans, who bore children to them. These were the heroes that were of old, warriors of reknown.
GENESIS 6:4

Oh! The Nephilim! Where have they gone? Who *were* they? Were they the Greek gods, maybe, carried to the Hebrews on wisps of legend, lodged safely in the distant past, so as not to injure the monotheism for which the Hebrews became the witnesses? They certainly act like them: mating with the daughters of human beings, siring godlike progeny. Maybe so: Maybe they were just a snatch of myth from another culture. Whoever the Nephilim were, we never hear of them again after this mention of them in Genesis.

Things went downhill fast, it seems. Soon nobody was a giant—nobody was any good at all, in fact, except Noah, but we know when his story begins that he will somehow triumph. That we will see a new creation after terrible destruction.

Why this story, so soon after the story of the creation? Why a second fall of humanity? Different strands of biblical tradition account for it, of course, but *someone* decided to include both tales in the same book, both testaments to human error and divine sternness, tempered with a later divine mercy. We get what's coming to us, all right, but there is always a way back home.

The Genesis stories: terrible reverses of fortune, deserved and undeserved, redeemed by God. Great obstacles surmounted. Magical giants no longer walk the earth—just us, frail and faulty. But God continues to work with us, and once again we are saved.

SATURDAY IN EPIPHANY I

Pss 20, 21:1–7 (8–14) * 110:1–5 (6-7), 116, 117
Genesis 6:9–22
Hebrews 4:1–13
John 2:13–22

After he was raised from the dead, his disciples remembered that he had said this; and they believed the scripture and the word that Jesus had spoken.

JOHN 2:22

We sometimes see this kind of adjustment in John's gospel—he re-reads his text and realizes that something doesn't sound right, and so he seeks to explain it away: People remembered this remark of Jesus' about rebuilding the temple later on, he says, and so now we know what Jesus meant.

John never wants Jesus to appear as anything less than amazing—he strides through the gospel like Superman. He is oracular in his pronouncements, and even in daily conversation. John knows, writing forty or fifty years after the event, that the temple has been destroyed for good—Jesus didn't put it back together in three days, and neither did anyone else. And yet the record showed that Jesus had said these words—what to do? Ah: He wasn't really talking about the temple. He meant the temple of his body. Oh. This is what we would call "spin" if it were being reported today. But John wrote a long time ago.

It is true that John's Jesus is so divine that it would be easy to miss his humanity altogether if this one were the only gospel we had. But it is not the only one—we have three others. We absorb a spectrum of early Christian experience in the four gospels the early Church chose to take along with us on the ride.

And besides, John's Olympian Jesus bears a closer look. His feet hardly ever touch the ground, it's true. But John's Jesus is also the only one—in all of the four gospels—who cries when his friend dies. Maybe he is more like us than he looks when we first meet him.

SUNDAY, EPIPHANY II

Pss 148, 149, 150 * 114, 115
Genesis 7:1–10, 17–23
Ephesians 4:1–16
Mark 3:7–19

Whenever the unclean spirits saw him, they fell down before him and shouted, "You are the Son of God!" But he sternly ordered them not to make him known.

MARK 3:11–12

The seventeenth-century poet John Milton described the fall of Satan from heaven as a matter of his choice—"Better to reign in Hell than serve in Heaven," he snarls, and down he goes, to plot against humanity for the rest of time. But his disobedience is permitted by God, who remains securely in charge: Satan doesn't act outside the scope of God's power and goodness in Milton. Whatever else one might say about the world, in Milton's view, its ultimate fate is not in doubt.

The demons in the New Testament agree. They fall down and worship Jesus, at the same time as they continue to torture their unfortunate victims.

Why do you suppose Mark wants us to know that even the demons know Jesus? Perhaps it is important to him that we be profoundly encouraged, changed by what has happened in Jesus' life and death. Remember that Mark is the one whose oldest versions don't include a resurrection appearance: just frightened disciples, as confused and scared as we are, running away from an empty tomb. Mark needed to get whatever confidence he had from the life of Christ: The meaning of his resurrection is not yet developed. And Mark had a lot of confidence: His gospel is breathless with excitement. And so the demons themselves proclaim him, in the very moment of their vanquishing: The very essence of uncleanness must acknowledge the mighty goodness of God.

MONDAY IN EPIPHANY II

Pss 25 * 9, 15
Genesis 8:6–22
Hebrews 4:14–5:6
John 2:23–3:15

As long as the earth endures, seedtime and harvest, cold and heat, summer and winter, day and night, shall not cease.
GENESIS 8:22

My rector drew our attention to this promise when we were studying for confirmation, and had us memorize it—we memorized everything in those days, and forty years later I can still come up with those old words. *Shall not cease*, he would intone in his rich baritone as he helped us learn it, and back came our little trebles in response: *Shall not cease!*

It was a reassuring thought. Those were the days when the end of the world seemed, often, to be distressingly near—we had dropped an A-bomb ourselves, and there didn't seem to be any compelling reason why one wouldn't fall on us any day now. People built fallout shelters in their back yards. We thought we might not live to see adulthood.

The rector was young himself—thirty-five, or so. I think he may have sensed the dread that nibbled away at us, that he may have known we were afraid. Or maybe not. All I remember is that I trusted him absolutely, and believed him when he told the story of God destroying a sinful world, and then regretting having done it. Never again. No matter how scary it got, God would allow the earth to continue.

I still believe that. I no longer think a human presence on the earth is integral to its survival, of course: The earth will remain, but we will not. We are her temporary guests.

That's okay. It was lovely to be invited at all.

TUESDAY IN EPIPHANY II

Pss 26, 28 * 36, 39
Genesis 9:1–17
Hebrews 5:7–14
John 3:16–21

I have set my bow in the clouds. . . .
GENESIS 9:13

Oh, look! I said, and then I was embarrassed—after all, I was an adult, riding the train to Philadelphia, in a car full of strangers. But it was too late; people raised their heads to look at me inquiringly. *A rainbow,* I explained a little sheepishly, pointing out the window on the left side of the car. And only a few of my fellow passengers resumed their newspapers or their naps: Most of them did what I had done, craned their necks to see the beautiful bow of colors stretch across the weary industrial landscape just north of Trenton.

It's a double, one man said, *see?* And so it was: two bands of rainbow, one on top of the other. *Wow*, I said. We watched the double rainbow until we left it behind to enter the 33rd Street station.

My first large project in life was a rainbow. I was three years old, and I made an enormous cartoon strip for my mother, pasting sheets of paper end to end with flour-and-water paste, a story about a little girl and her mother, outside hanging clothes on the clothesline and seeing a rainbow. I can see it still: the bands of color dripping into one another, the curly-haired little girl in her triangle skirt, her stick arms and legs, her mother a taller version of her.

A bow of color after a rain: magic. Every culture has thought them meaningful: something so lovely, a bridge so brilliant—it must lead somewhere. Light, refracted through drops of water—that's all they are.

Maybe. Maybe not.

Here is some gratuitous beauty for you, God said. *It's a sign that I haven't forgotten you.*

WEDNESDAY IN EPIPHANY II

Pss 38 * 119:25–48
Genesis 9:18–29
Hebrews 6:1–12
John 3:22–36

. . . for he gives the Spirit without measure.
JOHN 3:34

Just as you can't be a little bit pregnant—you either are or you aren't—so the Spirit does not come by degrees. We have all of it if we have any of it.

But then again, ask any mother: You're not the same woman three days after your due date, unable to remember the last time you saw your own feet, and you're not the same you were three days after you got the news of your impending motherhood. Much has changed.

The Spirit, also, is living, and it changes those in whom it dwells. We can groom ourselves, schooling ourselves to bear it with power and joy, just as a pregnant woman can eat well, exercise wisely, take her vitamins. We can avoid those things that impede the growth of the Spirit's life within us, as a pregnant woman can avoid tobacco, alcohol, and other drugs. And we can allow our hearts and minds to play over the possibility and promise that lives inside us. Just like an expectant mother, we can dream of the Spirit, and we are part of what we dream.

Eventually, a pregnant woman gives birth. It only seemed like years—it was really just nine months. And, eventually, the Spirit that lives in us and animates all our goodness outgrows our bodies. We become unable any longer to contain its strength. Eventually, it works its way free of us, in fear and pain, and it shoots with joy toward heaven.

THURSDAY IN EPIPHANY II

Pss 37:1–18 * 37:19–42
Genesis 11:1–9
Hebrews 6:13–20
John 4:1–15

"Are you greater than our ancestor Jacob . . . ?"
JOHN 4:12

A split-off group of the chosen people, the Samaritans. They worshipped the same God as the Jews but not, the Jews believed, in the proper way. Jacob, his well, his field, given to Joseph, the most beloved of his sons: These things all predate the entire experience of the Hebrews in Egypt. Predate Moses and the law. There was a relationship with God before the people of Israel received the law. Maybe some of the Samaritans never went to Egypt. And maybe others did, but returned to their ancestral lands and to some older customs and beliefs not endorsed in the book of Leviticus.

But close, nonetheless, the Samaritans and the Jews. About as close as the Palestinians are to the Israelis in the modern state. Much in common, but full to the brim with mutual mistrust.

Among many things for which Jesus had little time was ethnic suspicion and mistrust. He went repeatedly out of his way to demonstrate this, which is why it's so odd that *we* so often go out of *our* way to differentiate ourselves from people of other faiths and cultures. We talk of being a "Christian" nation, when we mean a moral one. Of "Christian values," meaning good ones. But many people besides Christians are moral and good.

FRIDAY IN EPIPHANY II

Pss 31 * 35
Genesis 11:27–12:8
Hebrews 7:1–17
John 4:16–26

It is beyond dispute that the inferior is blessed by the superior.
HEBREWS 7:7

Let us bless the Lord! I type in the dark, almost every morning. And people answer, hundreds of them lighting up the screen: *Thanks be to God!* I write in the early morning, usually, but some of them are on the other side of the world, and they receive my greeting at night. And some are just not morning people: If I check my e-mail at night, I am likely to find one or two stragglers. Sometimes they'll offer an explanation, but none is really needed. *It's always morning somewhere*, I write back, and beside, who says it has to be *Morning Prayer* anyway? Your prayer should be the prayer that works best for you.

If I am late, they greet me first. I notice that some of them put it a little differently, though. *Let us praise the Lord*, they write instead. I think they may feel a little presumptuous blessing the Lord, believing—with the writer to the Hebrews—that a blessing can flow only from God to me, not the other way around.

But it's not that kind of blessing. "Let us bless the Lord" does not confer on God anything he didn't already have. It is only an expression of thanks: *Bless you*, I might say, if you give me a drink of water when I am thirsty. *Bless you. Thanks.* And thanks back. Thanks and thanks: We agree.

The central message of "Let us bless the Lord" is gratitude. That is why it appears at the end of every one of the Daily Offices and almost every other service in the Prayer Book. Thanks for the day. Thanks the night. Thanks for the bread and for the wine, now body and blood for each of us. Thanks for the blessings.

SATURDAY IN EPIPHANY II

Pss 30, 32 * 42, 43
Genesis 12:9–13:1
Hebrews 7:18–28
John 4:27–42

*"Come and see a man who told me
everything I have ever done!"*
JOHN 4:29

Remember *This Is Your Life?* The show that aired a person's life story in front of God and everybody else, bringing back her aged mother and her childhood friends, his army buddy and his second-grade teacher for tearful on-air (and later, on-camera) reunions. Sometimes it was a celebrity's life the host invaded, and sometimes it was an ordinary Joe. The host would disguise himself—maybe as a waiter, or a salesman—and engage the victim in some innocent way, until the time came for him for him to shriek, *"JOHN SMITH, THIS IS YOUR LIFE!!!!!"* and the parade of auld acquaintance would begin.

Radio comedians Bob and Ray had a funny sketch satirizing the show: An emotionless guest was presented with people from his past, including a sister he hadn't seen in fifty years. The frantic host tried his manic best to elicit a touching exchange between the two, while it became clearer and clearer to everyone that they really weren't interested in each other at all. Finally the man said, *Well, I guess I'd better be getting back now.* And the sister said, *Yeah, me, too.* And that was the end of that.

I'd be embarrassed, I guess, if absolutely everyone I'd ever known came up on stage to surprise me. There are moments in my past I'd just as soon not relive. But the Samaritan woman with the colorful marital history found it a wonderful thing when Jesus told her about her life: accepted, healed, forgiven, *understood*, maybe for the first time ever. I imagine she was a bit of a joke in her small town. But she wasn't a joke to this stranger.

Our lives are not on stage, thank God. But we *are* known. Completely known, known even better than we know ourselves. It is lovely to think of being so known and yet so loved. Not embarrassing, not any more. Just lovely.

SUNDAY, EPIPHANY III

Pss 63:1–8 (9–11), 98 * 103
Genesis 13:2–18
Galatians 2:1–10
Mark 7:31–37

They asked only one thing, that we remember the poor,
which was actually what I was eager to do.
GALATIANS 2:10

Religious leaders always try and mostly fail to find doctrinal agreement. It's uncomfortable for them to admit that people just see things differently, and that this applies to the way they see

God as well. Why anybody would think it would be otherwise is a mystery to me, but there it is.

I just don't think we should get too worked up about the fact that good-hearted people can disagree about very important things. God will reveal what needs revealing, and we'll all remain puzzled about the rest. But what part of "remember the poor" don't we understand? And do we sometimes allow our lack of consensus about the things we will never be able to demonstrate or understand to suck valuable time and energy from the service we could be offering to those who need it?

What will happen if the Church splits apart like an egg over the issue of homosexuality? Well, that will be a pity. But it should not distract people who follow Christ, whatever they think about this or any other issue, from his clear call to focus on the poor and suffering in our midst.

The division between those who favored following the Jewish law and those who knew the Church could not spread in the non-Jewish world if that were required was every bit as bitter as the current struggle. Just as passionate. The stakes were just as high: the abandonment of a tradition that went back two thousand years and permeated every aspect of every Jew's life, from sunup to sunset and from birth to death. And we can learn from the leadership of the Church in those days: They were wise enough to allow this division to remain unresolved for a time, so that the good news could travel and the poor could be served.

MONDAY IN EPIPHANY III

Pss 41, 52 * 44
Genesis 14:(1–7) 8–24
Hebrews 8:1–13
John 4:43–54

When he came to Galilee, the Galileans welcomed him,
since they had seen all that he had done in Jerusalem
at the festival; for they too had gone to the festival.
JOHN 4:45

Now that Jesus is a genuine celebrity, the home folks suddenly find much in him to commend, and it turns out that everybody has always been his best friend. But we remember what happened the last time he tried to preach there.

Is there a person you remember from your youth who was the butt of everyone's jokes? Kids can be so cruel. Do you know what happened to him? To her?

One of the scapegoats in my high school ended up running for political office and winning. I remember the set of his chin as they tormented him, the way he didn't meet anyone's eyes, willing himself to just disappear, somehow, until it was over.

Nobody in the school then ever thought that this tortured boy was the most Christlike of all of us, but of course he was. He was the one persecuted by a mob for no good reason. He bore the insecurities of the other young people on his own defeated shoulders. It must have been terrible.

And yet—he was *not* defeated. Not at all. He survived his ignominy. The rest of his life rose from the tomb of his wounded pride and he became a prominent, successful adult. His adult self was nothing like his young self. I imagine that many of his tormentors did not go on to become as successful as he did, and I imagine that some of them became his friends, or wanted to be. Probably some of them tell themselves today that they have always been his friends—we don't usually remember our worst behavior nearly as well as we recall our best. So perhaps they have forgotten.

TUESDAY IN EPIPHANY III

Pss 45 * 47, 48
Genesis 15:1–11, 17–21
Hebrews 9:1–14
John 5:1–18

*Now that day was a sabbath. So the Jews said to the man
who had been cured, "It is the sabbath; it is not lawful
for you to carry your mat."*

JOHN 5:9–10

I imagine the audience, if there was one, howled with laughter at this part of the story: A well-known, lifelong invalid is miraculously cured, taking his first few hesitant steps—and his neighbors immediately criticize him for walking while carrying his mat on the Sabbath. They display something like *chutzpah*, I guess we'd call it, one of those *this-food-is-terrible-and-there's-not-enough-of-it* complaints.

There are people you simply can't please, and—after a good-faith effort—you shouldn't try. They want to be unhappy more than they want whatever it is that they claim to want. Don't deprive them of their complaints. That's all some people have. And there are institutions so focused on the details of their own arrangements that they no longer remember what ideal the details were created to protect. The Sabbath was supposed to be about the people taking time to rest and think of God's goodness. It's hard to think of a better way to do that than to see someone God had healed. But rules were rules.

Jesus has a good approach to rule-breaking: If you break a rule, know that you're doing it and have a good reason. Ordinarily, it's best to obey them. But once in a while, the greater good is served by doing something else. Don't expect the system that made the rules to back you up—you're probably on your own in your civil disobedience. So be clear yourself about what you have done and why: If it is of God, your action will produce something very good.

WEDNESDAY IN EPIPHANY III

Pss 119:49–72 * 49, (53)
Genesis 16:1–14
Hebrews 9:15–28
John 5:19–29

"Your slave-girl is in your power; do to her as you please."
GENESIS 16:6

Abraham is the one whose faith in God made him the patriarch of us all. It's important to remember, though, that his faith didn't protect him from sliding easily into the sins of his society—as in this instance, when he waves away the woman who has shared his bed and become pregnant with his child as just another piece of his wife's property. Neither Abram nor Sarai come off particularly well in this story. So the patriarchs aren't patriarchs because they're better or more morally fit than anyone else. They're patriarchs just because they're patriarchs: forebears who were in relationship with the God with whom we're in relationship, without whose experience with that God we would not have inherited what we have received.

It's interesting, though, that the writer doesn't convey any real disapproval of their cruel actions. God is kinder to Hagar and her child than are either Abram or Sarai, but they are not punished for their meannness. I guess the writer didn't think it was especially mean. It is only we who are shocked.

What are the things that we view with equanimity that will shock our descendants? What things will make them look at one another in disbelief and ask *How could they have done that?* There will be some: Perhaps it is our flaccid response to the reality of world hunger or our tolerance for repeated pandemics of preventable disease.

How could they have done that? The fullness of God's truth had not yet been revealed to them. How can we allow the things we allow? Whether we see it now or not, future generations will ask.

THURSDAY IN EPIPHANY III

Pss 50 * (59, 60) or 118
Genesis 16:15–17:14
Hebrews 10:1–10
John 5:30–47

You search the scriptures because you think that in them
you have eternal life; and it is they that testify on my behalf.
Yet you refuse to come to me to have life.
JOHN 5:39–40

But *don't you believe in the Bible?* a young woman asks me. She is
torn apart by her brother's revelation to the family that he is gay.
It's very *new* news; it's not clear at all, yet, how the family will deal
with it: what their father will say, their mother, their other brother.

Actually, she is not surprised. *I think I always sort of knew it*, she
says. *We used to double date together, but he was always just pals with
the girls he went out with. Always. We always just had a good time.*
And it really doesn't change the way she loves her brother. But the
family is a churchgoing one, and their pastor has been vocal from
the pulpit against gay marriage, so emphatically against it that their
father thinks he's gone around the bend. *I just wish he'd talk about
something else once in a while*, he said at dinner after church one
Sunday. But that was before her brother came out, which he did to
the members of his family separately on the same day: his parents
first, in person, then his siblings, one at a time, by telephone.

She knows her parents believe in the Bible. So does she. But she
can't quite get her mind around the idea that, all of sudden, her little brother is an abomination. That he ought to be stoned. She's
sure that can't be the case.

I'm pretty sure of that, too. I think God is free, and that the Bible
tells the story of humankind's journey through the world of experience to the world of spirit. The book reveals God, but God is not
imprisoned by the book. History develops, and God is part of history's development.

So yes, we believe in the Bible as God's revelation. And no, we don't believe in the Bible to the exclusion of God's freedom to act in history. This means we'll be uncertain, often, as we encounter new things, and also uncertain when we encounter old things in the pages of the ancient books that comprise Holy Scripture. It means we might make mistakes, and that a loving, living God will have to break into our lives and straighten us out.

FRIDAY IN EPIPHANY III

Pss 40, 54 * 51
Genesis 17:15–27
Hebrews 10:11–25
John 6:1–15

"There is a boy here who has five barley loaves and two fish. But what are they among so many people?" Jesus said, "Make the people sit down." Now there was a great deal of grass in the place; so they sat down, about five thousand in all. . . . When the people saw the sign that he had done, they began to say, "This is indeed the prophet who is to come into the world."

JOHN 6:9–10, 14

What sign? How was the feeding of all those people a sign? A sign of what? What was Jesus telling the people when he produced all that food from practically nothing?

Look at what's going on, he's saying. Leave your unfinished business in the realm of the unfinished. Focus on things that matter. We have work to do: learning, puzzling over parables and hard-to-digest ethical teachings. We must understand why it is the poor who are blessed, why the meek will inherit the earth, when we have always thought it was the strong. We must watch in amazement as 5,000 people are fed from one little boy's lunch, and come to grips with the fact that there is enough food if we will only share it out fairly. And then we must cry out in anguished disbelief as the One who teaches us these things is ripped from us and killed, by a world not yet ready for the meek to inherit it.

And we don't have much time in which to do these things. We don't have decades and decades in which to learn what it is to take up the cross and follow. We may not even have the remainder of this day, for tomorrow is promised to none of us. We must accept our peculiar meekness now, learn—now—not to fear poverty, so that we can seriously address the poverty of the world. We must learn to hunger for righteousness as much as we do for the current crop of toys.

And we have all we need to learn these things. We know everything we need to know to begin, and there are signs aplenty. Our failure is not failing to understand. It's choosing not to use what we know.

SATURDAY IN EPIPHANY III

Pss 55 * 138, 139:1–17 (18–23)
Genesis 18:1–16
Hebrews 10:26–39
John 6:16–27

So Sarah laughed to herself, saying, "After I have grown old, and my husband is old, shall I have pleasure?"
GENESIS 18:12

I can imagine what Sarah's laugh was like: It must have been a bitter laugh, the rough, hard laugh of someone for whom hope had long ago become a cruel joke. Sarah laughed out loud, but she kept her thoughts to herself. Their visitors could hear the thoughts of her heart, though, and the depth of her bitterness was obvious to them.

We never share the sorrows we think are beyond healing. Why open that can of worms? Mostly we keep busy, so as to distract ourselves from it. And that works pretty well, until somebody else happens to mention it—then we are caught off guard. If we can, we deny that it's an issue at all, not for us: *I don't have a broken heart. Not me. I really couldn't care less.*

That's what Sarah's bitter laugh said. But the silent thoughts of her heart were much softer: *Will I really know such happiness?* She couldn't help peeking again at her old hope, even as she rejected the power of anyone to bring it into being. So there was a war in Sarah, a war between bitterness and hope.

Will you receive the gift for which you have longed for so many years that your hope for it was gone long ago? You may and you may not. Sarah had a Plan B: the surrogacy relationship she offered Abraham in the form of her serving girl Hagar—as cruel as it seems to us now, the plan seems not to have raised an eyebrow in the ancient Middle Eastern circles that first heard these old stories. She set about finding another way to have a child.

God works out of evil to bring good. Brings hope from disappointment. Finds another way. The couple was ready to follow that other way. In the end, both ways bore fruit.

SUNDAY, EPIPHANY IV

Pss 24, 29 * 8, 84
Genesis 18:16–33
Galatians 5:13–25
Mark 8:22–30

"But who do you say that I am?"
MARK 8:29

The really important things in life simply cannot be decided by other people, no matter how much they may love you. You have to do it yourself.

Of course, you don't do it in a vacuum. Well-meaning parents with memories of being taken to Sunday school when they didn't want to go sometimes seek to compensate themselves for this bygone annoyance by keeping their own children in the dark about religion: *We want to let him make up his own mind when he's older,* they say, getting themselves neatly off the hook.

But ignorance is a poor platform from which to make decisions. Children and adults need to know the wisdom of the world before they can make decisions about its content. Many people have said many things about God in the course of history, and it's a good idea to have some sense of what at least some of those things have been, so as not to have to reinvent the wheel every time you try to think theologically. This is true even if you end up rejecting a good deal of it.

Seek the advice of history, soak up the wisdom of those you love and trust. It will still be true that the job of synthesizing it is yours alone. But at least you won't be starting from a deficit.

MONDAY IN EPIPHANY IV

Pss 56, 57, (58) * 64, 65
Genesis 19:1–17 (18–23) 24–29
Hebrews 11:1–12
John 6:27–40

Do not work for the food that perishes,
but for the food that endures for eternal life. . . .
JOHN 6:27

What do you suppose this is? Q asks me. I take the glass jar he holds out to me and study it. I hold it up to the light and think I detect a purple tinge to the dark liquid inside.

I think it's beet juice. But the beet juice, if that's what it is, doesn't look well: Something white and fuzzy clings to the wall of the glass jar. Moving quickly, I make it to the kitchen sink before Q can stop me, and it goes down the drain.

This is painful to Q. He hates to waste food. I, on the other hand, am quite sure that no substance you can no longer identify qualifies as food, not any more. Maybe there used to be beet juice in that jar, but it's a science experiment now. Something about mediums for growing a fungus at home, an experiment that could save somebody's life some day, say when we're traveling to Mars in a space ship and get really desperate.

You can't keep stuff forever, not even with a fancy refrigerator. You can't do *anything* we do here on earth forever: forever isn't something human beings can summon. We're all just here for a visit.

You can pour all your wit and all your energy into the struggle: first for survival, and then for the obvious trappings of success. For permanent things, and then for other things to keep your permanent things safe—insurance on your insurance.

But it's all going—down the drain, some of it, and the rest somewhere else. Hold what you have lightly, because you're going to have to let it go.

TUESDAY IN EPIPHANY IV

Pss 61, 62 * 68:1–20 (21–23) 24–36
Genesis 21:1–21
Hebrews 11:13–22
John 6:41–51

But Sarah saw the son of Hagar the Egyptian, whom she had borne to Abraham, playing with her son Isaac.
GENESIS 21:9

You know that the child Ishmael is understood to be the ancestor of the people of Islam—their tradition is that it was Ishmael, not Isaac, who narrowly escaped being sacrificed by his father, and Abraham is celebrated for his chilling obedience in that incident in the Muslim feast of Eid. Tradition also has it that Abraham and Ishmael built the Kaaba in the city of Mecca together. Ishmael is venerated in Islam as a prophet appointed by God.

So we're not very far apart at all. These ancient legends about Abraham have passed down in Muslim circles as well as in our own.

Here in Genesis we see the two little boys who share the same father playing together in peace, about to be interrupted in their happiness by the doings of the jealous adults around them. It seems to have begun early, this sibling rivalry. Too bad. The kids were fine: It was the adults who were worried about the inheritance. But the inheritance of God's love isn't in short supply. We're not going to run out of it. The more love you spend the more you have.

So I guess it isn't the limitless love of God the adults in this story fear losing. It's their sense of chosen-ness, of being the only ones to whom the divine love is given. At their unloveliest, Abraham and Sarah—especially Sarah, in this story—are all about their own privileged position, rather than about the inauguration of a covenant that would one day encompass the whole of humanity.

WEDNESDAY IN EPIPHANY IV

Pss 72 * 119:73–96
Genesis 22:1–18
Hebrews 11:23 31
John 6:52–59

After these things God tested Abraham.
GENESIS 22:1

Many writers have been haunted by this ancient story of a father willing to sacrfice the life of his only son. It might be one thing, we think, to make such a choice in the case of a terrible moral dilemma: What if I could save the lives of a great many people by sacrificing the life of my child? But this is different: Nobody else's life was at stake in this story. Nobody was in any danger that Isaac's death would avert. It was just a sacrifice to a god who, Abraham was sure, wanted the blood of his only child.

In the end, no. A ram appears: the human sacrifice is not to be. We read this ancient tale today, and realize that we are witnessing a change in the faith larger than one man's experience, though it is symbolized in this tale. This was the moment: An old sin took its place in the past.

THURSDAY IN EPIPHANY IV

Pss (70), 71 * 74
Genesis 23:1–20
Hebrews 11:32–12:2
John 6:60–71

"This teaching is difficult; who can accept it?"
JOHN 6:60

Then as now: If something is just too disturbing for us to bear, we try mightily to convince ourselves that it can't be true, so we can cross it off our list of things to worry about. That's pretty dangerous policy, but it's what we do.

Some beliefs are just too much work: They would require us to change so many other things that we'd alter the landscape of our lives beyond our recognition. The collision between our Founding Fathers' embrace of human equality and the fact that many of them were slaveholders is an example of that: They had to believe that changing society to a degree that would make the position of African Americans commensurate with their God-given equality with whites was economically impossible, that it would have been bad for everyone, that it would have been bad for the slaves themselves. If they had admitted it was possible, then they would have had to do it.

Individuals, too, evade truths that are just too hard to implement: It's much easier on me if I cling to the idea that God is uninterested in human affairs in general and my own life in particular. If I think that, there's no reason for me to concern myself with prayer, with puzzling about the things of God. An unpleasant fatalism is all that's required of me, and that comes with no effort on my part.

But I would also have to live with the meaninglessness of such a posture. With my own meaninglessness. As it is, I must ponder a God who accompanies us through our sorrows but does not cause them, who brings good out of evil that happens at random. It is a life's work.

But it is worth the trouble.

FRIDAY IN EPIPHANY IV

Pss 69:1–23 (24–30) 31–38 * 73
Genesis 24:1–27
Hebrews 12:3–11
John 7:1–13

*Before he had finished speaking, there was
Rebekah, who was born to Bethuel son of Milcah,
the wife of Nahor, Abraham's brother, coming
out with her water jar on her shoulder.*

GENESIS 24:15

Such an ancient story, a story of every culture: A man is looking
for a wife, and a young woman presents herself, seemingly by
accident. But we know it is meant to be. These two are even related.

We love to hear stories of people meeting and falling in love. We
even love telling our own stories of love, love lost and love found.
Even our loves are fascinating.

Do you think there's a soul mate for each of us? the young man
asks me. He is lonely, and longs to fall in love. One person we're
destined to love?

Hmmn. Destined? Only one person in the entire world, destined
for you from the beginning of time? Probably not. I think there are
probably many people with whom each of us could build a happy
life. We each bring the desire to love and the capacity to commit
ourselves to life together into love with us, and it is those things that
make love last. You each bring those things, and they bridge the gap
that occasionally appears between ideal and reality in every union.

Rebekah is beautiful and good, hard-working and hospitable,
obedient and yet possessed of personal initiative. She's a good match
for her cousin Isaac. But both of them also know exactly what is
expected of them, and we are watching them prepare to pledge
themselves to it. They'll be fine.

SATURDAY IN EPIPHANY IV

Pss 75, 76 * 23, 27
Genesis 24:28–38, 49–51
Hebrews 12:12–29
John 7:14–36

"How does this man have such learning,
when he has never been taught?"
JOHN 7:15

Well, we don't learn everything we need to know in school. These days you need a diploma to enter a profession—a piece of paper given only to people who have successfully completed a certain course of study: If you have such a document, presumably, you have done that work. The paper stands for a body of learning.

Of course, a person could accumulate that learning in another way. You could just read books on your own, and talk to people. Then you'd need to demonstrate that you possessed the same knowledge as a person who has a diploma. You'd take a test. Maybe a group of diplomates would examine you, and maybe they would certify that you were as learned in the field as you needed to be. If you were, then you'd get the diploma: a kind of shorthand for evidence of your learning.

In almost every field today, the second, less formal method of acquiring knowledge is insufficient. You need the piece of paper, and your progress without it will be difficult and slow. Perhaps it will be impossible.

Our faith in credentials is pretty complete: It's hard for us to look beyond them. Certain schools we deem better than other schools, and we want to hire people who went to those schools. We are so comfortable with the authority of credentials that we don't always check to see if the one holding them really does know what the paper says he does. Whether he is wise or not.

Jesus is unschooled, but he is not untaught. The authority with which he teaches is immediately evident, and that is what puzzles the rabbis: He's not fitting properly into their template. A credential is a handy shorthand for anyone's wisdom, but it does not guarantee that it is present. And the absence of credentials might just be the same, sometimes. There is no substitute for discovering one another's wisdom the old way: by discovering one another.

SUNDAY, EPIPHANY V

Pss 93, 96 * 34
Genesis 24:50–67
2 Timothy 2:14–21
Mark 10:13–22

*Remind them of this, and warn them before God that
they are to avoid wrangling over words, which does
no good but only ruins those who are listening.*
2 TIMOTHY 2:14

Why isn't this verse embroidered on altar frontals and polychromed over sanctuary entrances? Why doesn't it appear anywhere on my seminary diploma? Think of the trouble we could have spared ourselves.

I am trying to recall the number of times I have seen someone convinced by an argument about words. Hardly any: People just talk at each other and then they get mad and go away. And yet we love to do it, want the clarity we would gain from agreement about what exactly we meant by this or that, when truth and reconciliation almost always come about in another way: We move toward them slowly, through weighing our experience and hearing the experience of others, through talking and studying and, yes, arguing. But we rarely achieve it just by arguing. And the more common experience we have together, the more productive and the shorter our argument will be.

I'm a writer; I love words. But they can't sustain the weight of a spiritual life all by themselves. You haven't finished with *anything* when you have understood it intellectually and think you've dispatched all its ambiguities. You've only just begun.

MONDAY IN EPIPHANY V

Pss 80 * 77, (79)
Genesis 25:19–34
Hebrews 13:1–16
John 7:37–52

Keep your lives free from the love of money,
and be content with what you have. . . .
HEBREWS 13:5

All you have to do is click, and you can buy anything—sheets, diamonds, stocks, cars. More sheets with more thread counts in more colors and more patterns than you knew existed. More cars and stocks and diamonds and records, more cigarettes and prescription drugs, probably, than really need to exist. Certainly more than anyone needs.

Or you can turn on the television late at night and watch people discuss things to buy. They hold them up to the camera so we can examine them at great length. How much can a person say about a vegetable slicer? A lot more than one might think.

And if there were a fire? What would you carry out? The vegetable slicer? The stereo? And, when the insurance claim was settled, would you go out and buy it all again: more vegetable slicers? More sheets?

No. We would make sure the people were all out. And the animals. We would try to grab our wallets and the photographs of those who have died, and maybe we would get them all and maybe we wouldn't. All the rest would go up in flames and we would stand and watch, our backs cold from the cold street and our fronts hot from the hot fire, and we would think *Thank God. Thank God we're alive.*

Be content with what you have. Who knows? It could be all you ever have. You never know when you might suddenly have to make do with much less. Best not to let either your riches or your poverty define who you are.

TUESDAY IN EPIPHANY V

Pss 78:1–39 * 78:40–72
Genesis 26:1–6, 12–33
Hebrews 13:17–25
John 7:53–8:11

*Now may the God of peace, who brought back from the
dead our Lord Jesus, the great shepherd of the sheep, by the
blood of the eternal covenant, make you complete in
everything good so that you may do his will, working
among us that which is pleasing in his sight. . . .*

HEBREWS 13:20–21

These words from the letter to the Hebrews form the blessing given those who mourn at the end of the Burial Office. We are still here, even after a terrible loss. God will still work with us and form us. We will be given what we need to get through the lonely days ahead.

We will also use it as a blessing during the Easter season. Easter and funerals: They are the same. The altar hangings and priests' vestments are white, or even festal: beautiful and bright, whatever the season of the year. In the dead of winter or the week after Christmas or in the dark of Lent, even when it's bitter cold and snow is on the ground: flowers, a candle symbolizing the resurrection. And words about the work yet to be done, about reasons for living here on the earth, even after you have lost that without which you thought you could not live.

We will still be pleasing in the sight of God. And, because God loves us, being pleasing in God's sight means being joyful. We will not be joyful in the same way, not exactly. How could we—our beloved isn't among us in the same way. Nothing will be exactly the same as if was before; nothing ever is. But there will still be goodness, and we will re-learn how to recognize and feel it.

We come and go on the earth. We don't stay long. We hate our leaving—even those of us who hope for heaven still hate to leave the earth. But the shepherd who led us here leads us there, and we are never lost.

WEDNESDAY IN EPIPHANY V

Pss 119:97–120 * 81, 82
Genesis 27:1–29
Romans 12:1–8
John 8:12–20

*We have gifts that differ according to
the grace given to us. . . .*
ROMANS 12:6

An extraordinary number of people make early educational choices according to what their parents want them to do. Your dad wants you to be the engineer he never got to be. Your mother was a teacher, and you know she'd love it if you were a teacher, too. Your father is the third in a line of priests; he and your grandfather are always talking about your going to their seminary, as if it were a foregone conclusion that you *will* go. And maybe their paths really are the paths for which you are suited. Good.

But maybe they are not. Life is getting longer all the time, they tell us, but it's still too short to do what someone else did, or what someone else wishes she had done, instead of that to which you are called. Every job deserves to be done with seriousness and devotion. It's hard to be devoted to a job for which you are unsuited.

Are you no longer young? Are you caught in a profession you now know was never really yours, and now it's too late? Now you're vested in your pension, established in your children's schools, your spouse's career, your neighborhood? In too deep to get out?

God always has a way to work. The divine purpose never has only one means to its ends; it always has several spares. If we missed the bus the first time, there's always another bus. And now you have the advantage of maturity, the wisdom of years, the courage that comes from knowing that few things are really irrevocable. You're not too old to make a new beginning, not if you can remain flexible and not insist that it be the same beginning it would have been if you have done it when you were twenty-three. You're not too old to begin until you're dead, and God isn't even finished with you then.

THURSDAY IN EPIPHANY V

Pss (83) or 146, 147 * 85, 86
Genesis 27:30–45
Romans 12:9–21
John 8:21–32

Do not lag in zeal. . . .
ROMANS 12:11

Perhaps my nails need a polish—yes, they do. How about that? All twenty of them could use some attention, a task that will delay my starting to write by a good twenty minutes. After that, I suppose I'll have to think of something else.

I love to write. Really, I do. Nothing feels as good as seeing the words follow one another on the page with an elegance that surprises me. For years I whined to anyone who would listen about not having the large blocks of time a writer needs. But now that I have it, I am forever shooting it in the foot, placing unnecessary tasks ahead of my deadlines. I sit down to write and immediately feel like baking something. Straightening something. Calling someone about something that really could wait.

Some of the things we love are like that, especially the things we love that are also a lot of work: It takes awhile to get into the *zone*, that place where time just goes away, where you are so focused on your work and love it so much that you don't really care about much else. Four, five hours can pass, a bright afternoon turn into a dark night, and you don't even notice.

At the end of a day like that, you're tired. A little exercise then, to get the kinks out. A dinner reunion with your spouse, who's been absorbed in his own work all day. A nice bath, maybe and some good-night prayer. The days on which I treat my zeal with respect and love are wonderful days. God must have made us for this.

FRIDAY IN EPIPHANY V

Pss 88 * 91, 92
Genesis 27:46–28:4, 10–22
Romans 13:1–14
8:33–47

*"I am weary of my life because
of the Hittite women."*
GENESIS 27:46

Well, we know that feeling, don't we? Aren't there people whose unexpected appearance in the midst of your day just makes your heart sink? Not that they're not children of God and all that— it's just that we adore some of God's children and can survive a long time between visits from some of the others.

Of course, Rebekah's objection was to all the Hittite women, not just the annoying ones. That's a little different. It was a longing for home and kindred, I guess—the same longing that had seized Abraham when he sent for her so long ago as a bride for his son. But it is that same understandable longing—who does not long for home?—that undergirds all the racial and ethnic miseries the world has ever seen, and the world has seen a lot of them.

We must find a way to love our own people and honor our own past while, at the same time, we rise to the challenge of honoring the neighbor who is not one of us. Our history of doing that is a sorry one. Love of family and tribe and country translates much too smoothly into suspicion of the outsider. The world is too small for that to work.

And we make it smaller, still, by closing ourselves off from any but our own. Smaller and less robust—pedigree animals are notoriously delicate: too much inbreeding. We strengthen the only race that really exists—the human race—by doing what Rebekah refused to do: mixing things up a little.

SATURDAY IN EPIPHANY V

Pss 87, 90 * 136
Genesis 29:1–20
Romans 14:1–23
John 8:47–59

So Jacob served seven years for Rachel,
and they seemed to him but a few days. . . .
GENESIS 29:20

I counted it up, my friend said glumly. *If I keep taking courses at the rate I'm taking them now, it'll take me eight years to finish college.* She sounded so discouraged. Eight years is a long time.

On the other hand, I said, she still had to live those eight years. They would pass whether she went to school or not: it's not as if taking classes would lengthen those years and not going would shorten them. They'd be eight years whatever she did. She'd still be eight years older at the end of them, no matter what. The only difference would be that she'd be eight years older with a college degree if she went to school and eight years older without one if she didn't.

Things seem so long before we begin them. The prize at the end of a long effort is a million miles away when you look forward to it: *I'll never get there.* But we live each day at a time, and when it is over, it is gone forever. Life is one day closer to being over, no matter what we do.

And now, look back: over your years of education, your years of ministry. Of marriage, of working, of child-rearing. Twenty, thirty, forty years gone, in what seems like the twinkling of an eye. You used to think thirty years was a long, long time. And now? Now it seems like nothing at all.

SUNDAY, EPIPHANY VI

Pss 66, 67 * 19, 46
Genesis 29:20–35
1 Timothy 3:14–4:10
Mark 10:23–31

"Surely now my husband will love me."
GENESIS 29:32

These people lived a long time ago, but Leah could have said these painfully hopeful words earlier this afternoon. How many women have thought a baby would "bring us together"?

Nope. You'd better be together before the little one arrives. Besides being wonderful, babies are stressful and a lot of work. It's a long time before they exist for anyone but themselves, and they don't negotiate their needs. They don't come into your family to help you stay married. They don't come into your family to help *you* do anything. You're going to have to help *them* for a long time.

One of the things that sticks in our throats about the world these ancient texts show us is the way some people are valued only insofar as they are useful to others. Women, for instance: so few of what we call "rights." Hardly any.

Slaves. Foreigners. Even children—all accessories to the powerful men in these stories. But look just under the narrative: The women are busy, planning, arranging, scheming for justice where no justice is to be expected. Even children in these ancient books use their wits to compensate for their weakness: In just a little while, we will see the young Miriam think quickly and save her brother. Innocent wit does battle with the mighty status quo. And just often enough to keep us hopeful, it comes out on top.

MONDAY IN EPIPHANY VI

Pss 89:1–18 * 89:19–52
Genesis 30:1–24
1 John 1:1–10
John 9:1–17

*"You must come in to me, for I have hired you
with my son's mandrakes."*
GENESIS 30:16

Well, *okay*, Jacob must have said. It doesn't sound like he had a lot of choice: Leah had rented him for the night from Rachel for a bunch of mandrake roots. The mandrake root is an amusingly anthropomorphic part of a plant like ginseng—it looks like a human figure, and I suppose if you hold it just so, it also looks—well, *anatomically correct*. People in ancient times considered the plant a sexual aid, and Jacob probably could have used one from time to time.

Don't be so bemused by the mandrake that you overlook how tough Leah is on Jacob: He has no say in whom he sleeps with on that night, it seems. He comes in from the field, hot and sweaty and tired after a long day's hard work and the women have plans for him—and they are *orders*, their plans, not requests. In this little story, Jacob has all the authority of a stud stallion: lots of force, but not much autonomy. It just goes to show you: Human beings, even oppressed ones like almost all the women in the Bible, will find ways to exercise power.

The mandrakes seem to have worked their magic: Leah has three more children in rapid succession, just for old time's sake. And even the beloved but barren Rachel conceives at last.

How intent they are upon having children, all these people who lived so long ago! So willing to share intimacies we would not wish to share, to enter into humiliating bargains, to promise terrible things to a God they think might somehow be moved by their vows to hear their longing and act. They will go anywhere and do anything.

They are passionate beings—I don't mean just passionate in bed, for we don't know what goes on there in anybody's lives but our own, but passionate in their pursuit of that which they value above all else. They know what they want. They do not share our modesty about asking for their heart's desires, or even demanding them. They show no shame about all their scheming and skullduggery: All is fair, it seems.

And—God doesn't punish them for being so passionate. He works with them in the culture they inhabit, with their ways and their morals.

Remember that next time someone accosts you earnestly about how much better it would be if we conducted our relationships according to "biblical principles." I'd find out just which ones he meant before I'd agree to anything.

TUESDAY IN EPIPHANY VI

Pss 97, 99, (100) * 94, (95)
Genesis 31:1–24
1 John 2:1–11
John 9:18–41

Whoever says, "I am in the light," while hating
a brother or sister, is still in the darkness.
1 JOHN 2:9

Jesus knew this: In the collection of teachings we know as his Sermon on the Mount, he identifies hatred as the beginning of murder. You don't get too far in the project of killing for Christ before bumping into the brick wall of Jesus' life-affirming love. Even from the cross, he was able to look down upon his tormentors and understand them.

So you just can't hate people. Period. No matter who or why.

My friend lost her son at the World Trade Center. *I'm so glad you said what you said in your sermon,* she told me at lunch. *You called the men who did this murderers, not martyrs.*

And they *were* murderers. They were certainly not martyrs: They accomplished no good for their cause by their own deaths and they took thousands of people with them. Martyrs choose death only for themselves, never for someone else.

She went on to tell me about a sermon she had heard shortly after the attack, in which the preacher called for love instead of hate for those who perpetrated that terrible deed, as a way of ending the cycle of violent retribution. *I got up and walked out*, she said. *I mean, they killed my son.*

Each of us mourns in our own way, and can't reasonably be expected to interrupt that sad process in response to an ethical call until such time as it becomes possible to do so. Perhaps others can be reconcilers on the stricken mother's behalf—she has all she can do to get through each day.

Is her hatred akin to murder? I am not sure. I know she might be glad to murder her son's killers herself, if they were not already dead. Oh, yes, I think most of us can understand that feeling. Perhaps we can look at her hatred instead as an inevitable part of her terrible wound, something whose healing will happen in God's time and can't be predicted or pushed by anyone else.

WEDNESDAY IN EPIPHANY VI

Pss 101, 109:1–4 (5–19) 20–30 * 119:121–144
Genesis 31:25–50
1 John 2:12–17
John 10:1–18

The thief comes only to steal and kill and destroy.
JOHN 10:10

Iknew a man who had committed a violent crime. Knew him well—I was the employer who gave him a chance, invested a lot of time and attention in him. He was funny and intelligent. He looked like a person who was going to make good use of the two degrees he had earned at Sing Sing. I was in awe of someone who could do that.

As it happened, his story did not have a happy ending: Education can't cure everything, and his demons were fiercer than anyone knew—he is currently incarcerated again, for several rapes.

And you were alone with him? people asked. Yes, many times. I liked him very much—loved him, really. It broke my heart to see him begin to descend into his old darkness, even though I ended up being the victim of it and was truly frightened of him at the last.

I think of him now, back in Sing Sing. I know he is reading a lot, for that is his great love. He is, I think, a person who can only manage life in the strict confines of a prison environment; too much freedom didn't work for him.

But for my part, I don't begrudge a dime of the tax money we spent in giving him an education. In making a mind as good as it could be. Even if it was also most sadly diseased.

THURSDAY IN EPIPHANY VI

Pss 105:1–22 * 105:23–45
Genesis 32:3–21
1 John 2:18–29
John 10:19–30

Deliver me, please, from the hand of my brother. . . .
GENESIS 32:11

You've never made amends. Somehow years passed, and you went on with your life. You rarely saw the person with whom you clashed. Now it's been forever, and suddenly you know you're going to see him: at a wedding, at a funeral, at a reunion, at a retirement dinner. Oh, no. What will he say? What will I say? Who will speak first? What if he doesn't speak to me at all? You almost don't go, but you know you have to.

Jacob had tricked his brother Esau and it had cost Esau dearly. Of course, that was a long time ago. Maybe Esau had forgotten? No, probably not. But maybe he had forgiven Jacob? There was no way to tell until he got there.

Look at the elaborate strategy Jacob develops to manage his uncertain reception. He may hope for the best, but he prepares for the worst.

Whatever you must do to find your way back home, you will not be sorry you did. Maybe it will work out—maybe you'll stay there, picking up where you left off. Maybe bygones will be bygones. You won't know until you try. If you cannot restore the relationship, you have lost nothing—you were already estranged. And if you can, the years collapse into a moment, and the pair of you rejoice in finding each other again. It's worth the trouble and the fear.

FRIDAY IN EPIPHANY VI

Pss 102 * 107·1–32
Genesis 32:22–33:17
1 John 3:1–10
John 10:31–42

What we do know is this: when he is revealed we will
be like him, for we will see him as he is.
1 JOHN 3:2

I remember feeling shocked upon hearing about this ancient expectation for the first time: *We* will be like *Christ*? Live the life he lives? Decades of theological meekness had not taught me to hope for such a thing: "We are weak but He is strong," we used to sing, and I pictured Jesus Christ as so far above us in every way that the gulf between our states was infinite.

Ancient Christians found the idea just as shocking as I did. And that's the whole point: In Christ, two worlds that cannot meet become one reality. We're right to be shocked: This is a completely different view of new life from the one I had vaguely imagined for years, which was more or less a continuation of life as it is here on earth, except that everything works. But no. Resurrection brings something new to us, not just an eternity of something old.

All of our lives will end, but the kingdom of God does not end. In that domain, there is no time. Our lives, our deaths, our history—all are contained in it, but none of them *contain* it. Its limitlessness is beyond our limits and when we enter that domain, our limits disappear, too. We cease to be ourselves alone. We are in Christ. We are part of that kingdom now, already, though our experience of being part of it is severely limited: We can barely see it.

So maybe it is *not* so new. Maybe it has always been, and it is we who have not seen it. Maybe it's from outside history, and we can't sense it from our perch squarely within history's walls. And maybe we close our eyes to this world to open them to one we had forgotten we knew.

SATURDAY IN EPIPHANY VI

Pss 107:33–43, 108:1–6 (7–13) * 33
Genesis 35:1–20
1 John 3:11–18
John 11:1–6

. . . Jesus loved Martha and her sister and Lazarus. . . .
JOHN 11:5–6

This is one of the most comforting sentences in scripture. It meets us in that terrible place to which we all go sometimes: the place where we can't find God. The place where something has hurt us so much that it seems impossible to us that a God who knew about it would have allowed it to happen.

Funny—we were okay when it was *other* people hurting. Brought comfort to them, went to visit, made a casserole, shared the love we had and knew we were part of Christ's love in doing so. The existence of God and the love of God seemed everywhere then. It's only when it came to us that we felt so alone in the universe. But it isn't true that God doesn't love you when things go wrong. Things just go wrong in life sometimes.

Mary and Martha were surrounded by friends and neighbors when their brother died, we know. People with casseroles, people who came to visit. People who were there to do for them what they had done for others when somebody died. Living a life like that—a life in which you bring over a casserole when somebody dies—helps you remember sooner that God's love is not absent, even though your beloved is gone.

If you don't want to be isolated when heartache comes, don't be isolated beforehand. Learn the life of love early, learn to give it to others yourself, before your own heartache happens, and you will recognize it sooner. Lazarus came back from the dead, something our dear ones will not do. But he must have died again, right? He's not still around—he was raised from the dead to live life longer and then died—again. People again came to visit, brought a casserole, silently shared their love with those who remained. And now Mary and Martha knew more about what was ahead. Knew that we meet the beloved dead again, in another way. Knew their friend Jesus as the living Christ who never left them. They were still bereaved, but what they had learned the first time made all the difference in the world.

SUNDAY, EPIPHANY VII

Pss 118 * 145
Proverbs 1:20–33
2 Corinthians 5:11–21
Mark 10:35–45

Then they will call upon me, but I will not answer. . . .
PROVERBS 1:28

It sounds so mean when it is given voice in the allegorical character of Wisdom, but it is true: We *can't* produce wisdom all at once, when we need some, if we haven't developed any beforehand. Wisdom comes to us slowly, distilled from daily experience, keen observation, trial and error, over the course of a lifetime. We all need to make these investments, or wisdom will be in short supply when we need her most.

And nobody can do it for us. Warn your children as best you can, but they will not learn from your experience. They can only learn from their own. Nothing is harder than having to stand there watching as they skate too close to the edge, but somehow the consequences of their actions must become something more to them than hearsay.

The good news is how quickly and efficiently we *can* learn from experience, once we realize how important it is that we do so. Get in between others and the natural consequences of their actions as seldom as you can: Each time you cushion a blow for them, they lose a chance to learn.

I know a mother whose teenaged daughter had her fit to be tied. She had tried everything: nagging, pleading, therapy, lessons in this and that, reward and punishment—nothing made her daughter attend to her own future and take responsibility for her own actions. It looked to the mother as if the girl's chances for making it in the world were next to nothing.

So she gave up. There was nothing left to try. Almost immediately, the girl enrolled herself in secretarial school and graduated at the top of her class. She got a good job, and then a better one, and then a better one. She went to college and graduated with honors.

She needed to acquire wisdom herself. Her mom couldn't do it for her. Couldn't give it to her. She had to *pursue* it. And wisdom began to be hers, the moment she started her quest.

MONDAY IN EPIPHANY VII

Pss 106:1–18 * 106:19–48
Proverbs 3:11–20
1 John 3:18–4:6
John 11:17–29

The Lord by wisdom founded the earth. . . .
PROVERBS 3:19

The American textbook wars must seem strange to people from other countries—a school district somewhere in the South just went to court and lost its bid to require schools to affix a sticker to each science textbook stating that evolution is not a fact but a *theory*. As if all scientific propositions weren't theories. Dear me.

Talk of God's wisdom in forming the earth, does not, it seems to me, tell us much one way or another about how God might have gone about it. We narrow the scope of God's power when we insist that everything about him must make propositional sense or be journalistically true. We can't reduce God to a fact. Facts are just the beginning of truth. There is much more to it.

Maybe we'd do better if we approached puzzles like the creation of the world less in terms of knowledge and more in terms of love. For people of faith, the great gift of the creation stories in scripture is the love of God that the earth shows forth in its beauty, the meaning God's goodness gives to everything that is. These things far outweigh the science of it, if one's goal is to know God through the creation. And then, when God's goodness bursts upon our sight, the wonders science *can* unfold fill us with unambiguous awe.

We need never feel guilty about knowledge. We are created wanting to know. We just need to ask the right questions. In the right places.

TUESDAY IN EPIPHANY VII

Pss (120), 121, 122, 123 * 124, 125, 126, (127)
Proverbs 4:1–27
1 John 4:7–21
John 11:30–44

"Lord, if you had been here, my brother would not have died."
JOHN 11:32

I wonder how long it took Mary to realize that what she had just said made no sense. Did she think Jesus' presence meant that no one would ever die again?

But then again, the story we know so well had not unfolded for her, not yet. The crucifixion and resurrection were still in the future. So she didn't know what lay ahead. This miracle-working teacher was like no one else; maybe Mary really *did* think there would be no more death in the world because of his presence in it.

After all, we know people who *do* know the story, who wear crosses around their necks to remind them of Jesus' sacrifice, and *still* think that being a good Christian will somehow earn them a pass on the sorrows of life. After all that has happened to the faithful over the centuries, it's a mystery that anyone would still think this, but we know people who do. *What did I do to deserve this?* they ask anyone who will listen. Nothing. *Where is God in all this pain?* Where he's always been: right beside you, with his arm around your shoulder.

Arm? God doesn't have arms. But Jesus did, and the risen Christ embraces us all throughout our lives and straight into our deaths and beyond. Up from the grave comes Lazarus, that remarkable day—and some years later, on a day not recorded in any gospel, he will die again. On both days, the days we live and the day we die, Jesus is there.

LET US BLESS THE LORD

WEDNESDAY IN EPIPHANY VII

Pss 119:145–176 * 128, 129, 130
Proverbs 6:1–19
1 John 5:1–12
John 11:45–54

Go to the ant, you lazybones; consider its ways, and be wise.
Without having any chief or officer or ruler, it prepares its
food in summer, and gathers its sustenance in harvest.

PROVERBS 6:6–8

Lazybones? It certainly has a contemporary ring. The older
Revised Standard Version chooses "sluggard," as do the New
International Version and the King James and the New American
Standard Version and the New English Bible and the Jerusalem
Bible. Only the New Revised Standard is afraid we won't know what
a sluggard is. But I think anybody could tell, just by the sound: *slug-
gard*. What else *could* it mean?

I feel as if I were lazy, although nobody who knows me can understand why: *You run around from pillar to post every day, you do a
dozen different things at once. How can you possibly think you're lazy?*

But I am lazy inside, I say, *it doesn't show on the outside*. I am not
like the ant, who works along busily without an external authority to
force the issue: I must have a deadline, a due date, something outside
of me, something that measures me and grades my performance.
Don't tell me to take my time: I will. Give me a deadline to worry
about: Even if I miss it, I still need it in order to finish. It can be an anxious way to live, but it seems to be the only way I can be productive.

How lovely to be an ant, a little animal whose choices are so simple: Carry that crumb all the way back to the hill, even if it's bigger
than you are. Share it with the other ants. Eat all you can and save
the rest. To be programmed to do what you're supposed to do. And
how unnerving to be human, never sure if you will do what you say
you will do, if you will get it all done, if you will do it on time, if it
will be good enough.

Or, at least, that's how we think about ants. But maybe they're not as simple as we think they are. Maybe there are things about ants we don't know. And maybe we ourselves, whose intelligence is certainly antlike in comparison with the wisdom of our creator, maybe we are more programmed than we know. Perhaps we needn't worry so much about our work. Maybe our work is part of who we are, like the ant's work is part of her, and maybe God has already taken care of it.

Have a good day. Get as much done as you can, and know that the rest will be there tomorrow. There will always be more to do, and you will never finish. That's okay. It's just the way we are.

THURSDAY IN EPIPHANY VII

Pss 131, 132, (133) * 134, 135
Proverbs 7:1–27
1 John 5:13–21
John 11:55–12:8

"You always have the poor with you,
but you do not always have me."
JOHN 12:8

The rigor of Jesus' spiritual balance is a little unsettling here: Surely we're never supposed to miss a chance to serve the poor?

Those who work with the homeless burn out quickly if they don't have a place to go to refuel. Is it fair, that they have a place and their people do not? No. It is not fair at all. But they need to be able to give what they have to give, and if they allow themselves to be sucked dry of every morsel of energy they possess, they will have nothing with which to serve those most in need. Then it will be over. And so they must get a break, knowing as they head out of town that those for whom they work and pray never get one.

Love and work—Sigmund Freud said that these are the two things people need. The disciples knew a fair amount about the work, it seems, but love is always more confusing: It is at once strong and fragile, it both gives and requires energy. It fills us with joy and fear at the same time: joy at having it and fear of losing it.

We can never lose the love of God, but it does demand our presence in order for us to experience it. We must pay it some attention, or we won't *know* about it. Mary would have all her life to serve the poor, and we do, too. Sometimes, though, we must turn aside and pay attention to the God whose love has joined us to them in the first place.

FRIDAY IN EPIPHANY VII

Pss 140, 142 * 141, 143:1–11 (12)
Proverbs 8:1–21
Philemon 1–25
John 12:9–19

*All the words of my mouth are righteous;
there is nothing twisted or crooked in them.*
PROVERBS 8:8

Before we preach a sermon, we often pray that our words will be acceptable to God. At the start of a meeting, we pray over our deliberations, asking for wisdom and tact—I always used to pray for brevity, as well, a prayer not always granted. In praying with someone for healing on behalf of someone else, I usually ask that the words of my prayer partner be the words of Christ. *Give her your words, and let everything she says be from you.*

Words are potent: They can build up or tear down. We read in Genesis that it was with words that God created everything that is, and need not have a literal approach to scripture to see the blend of power, love, and will that moved upon faceless chaos and brought forth existence. And we know about the tearing down: How many times has a word escaped me that I would have given anything to call back? How many times have I cut someone with something sharper than it needed to be? Too many times to count.

I will count to ten before I speak, I tell myself each time. That's a good idea—ten seconds is long enough to get back in touch with what I really want to happen, to step back from a shotgun response and its deadly fallout. Now if I can just remember to do it.

Besides counting to ten, though, I could do the same thing with myself that I do with someone else who wants to pray for the sick: Ask Christ to speak through me. *Give me your words. Let everything I say be from you.*

SATURDAY IN EPIPHANY VII

Pss 137:1–6 (7–9), 144 * 104
Proverbs 8:22–36
2 Timothy 1:1–14
John 12:20–26

. . . unless a grain of wheat falls into the earth and dies, it remains just a single grain; but if it dies, it bears much fruit.
JOHN 12:24

I hear that the American life expectancy is going to be well over one hundred soon. Already, the number of centenarians has increased dramatically. So I guess a hundred will be the new eighty in a little while. "Old" will mean something other than what it means now—it already means something other than what it used to mean.

This idea makes me feel a little tired. Ready for a nap. *How* long do we have to stay here? We don't get any rest until *when*?

I object. It's not fair to the next generation for all of us to hang around forever and ever, and they can't take over until we move on. We had our turn and we need to let them have theirs, without us hovering in the background and looking over their shoulders.

Death came early in Jesus' time—life expectancy was short. Forty-five was old. Everyone knew it. From an early age, everybody knew what it was to mourn.

But stop and think a minute, Jesus says. Remember that what lies beyond this life you hate to leave is also good. That it is better, even—larger, less bounded by the things that bind you here. Don't struggle and struggle to stay here, as if *here* were the only place there is, for it is not. Not at all. *Here* is just the beginning of what is to be—and what is to be is here already.

SUNDAY, EPIPHANY VIII

Pss 146, 147 * 111, 112, 113
Proverbs 9:1–12
2 Corinthians 9:6b–15
Mark 10:46–52

The one who sows bountifully will also reap bountifully.

2 CORINTHIANS 9:6b

Here's how you manage to give money away: You do it first. Even if it's a small amount. Before you pay your other bills. You give what you have decided to give—you and your spouse, if you have one—and you do it first. Subsequent appeals will have to wait until the next time you decide; they can get in line. You decide at a time other than the time you write out the check—beforehand. That way, you're never ambushed and you never act on impulse and regret it later.

When you give first, you have enough. Perhaps our awareness of other people's needs makes us more moderate in our own consumption—I don't know. Time and again, though, purse-strings that were a very tight fit somehow have eased a little, stretched just enough to accommodate my obligations, and at the end, I have sat and looked at my checkbook in wonder: I did it, if just barely. And I've already given my gift. I gave it first. The check had already cleared before I had written out the last ones for all the bills.

The spiritual practice of giving first is no inoculation against your own foolishness—if you don't stick to what you've decided to do, the magic of giving will not make up your shortfall at the end.

But doing it first fills you with a sense of well-being and satisfaction. *I am a person who can give. A person richly blessed. I will somehow find a way to manage everything else.*

Was your gift bountiful? It was if you gave it first—if it came off the top, at the moment when your whole paycheck sat gleaming temptingly in the bank. When you could have done anything else with it.

MONDAY IN EPIPHANY VIII

Pss 1, 2, 3 * 4, 7
Proverbs 10:1–12
2 Timothy 1:15–2:13
John 12:27–36a

No one is crowned without competing according to the rules.
2 TIMOTHY 2:5

My friend is tired and discouraged. He is also angry: *Those people say they want to grow, but they don't want to change to do it,* he says as he slumps in his chair. *I'm supposed to get different results from doing exactly what they've always done!*

He hasn't been in the parish very long—less than a year. He came in with great ideas about what they might do together to help the place grow, and he was very open about those ideas in the process of interviewing. They saw some of the same things they're protesting now in action—and working well—when they visited him in his old parish. *They seemed so open to things,* he says. *I don't get it.*

You have to pay your dues, and having paid them in full somewhere else doesn't help you in a new place. The fact is, *nobody* wants to change. *Everyone* wants to have his cake and eat it, too. Fear of change is all about trust, and it is amazing how stubborn the fear of trusting the judgment of another is, how people cling ferociously to this or that detail or practice, how fiercely they defend their turf. Even if they said they wanted to change, they didn't really know what it would mean to do so.

He should slow down a bit in his ambitions for his new church. Rome wasn't built in a day. Let them grow together for a while, in love and trust. He should learn to rejoice in what is, not fret over what has not yet been achieved, and to value with sincerity who his people are right now, rather than withholding his respect until they are what he thinks they should be. Give all of them time to love one another. There will be time for many new gifts in the future—gifts he wants for them right now, and some gifts he hasn't even thought of yet.

TUESDAY IN EPIPHANY VIII

Pss 5, 6 * 10, 11
Proverbs 15:16–33
2 Timothy 2:14–26
John 12:36b–50

*Although he had performed so many signs in
their presence, they did not believe in him.*
JOHN 12:37

How about that? We always think we'd have had an easy time following Jesus if only we'd been lucky enough to have walked the earth at the same time he did, but maybe not. Lots of people saw him and heard him preach, saw him perform miracles, maybe even saw him raise Lazarus from the dead, and didn't think he was the son of God.

He seemed to understand this. I don't judge anyone who hears my words and doesn't keep them, he says. I'm here to save, not to judge. Part of coming among us was embracing our failure to follow, and loving us in spite of it. I guess he didn't hold it against us any more than we hold our teenagers' poor judgment against them. They're kids, we say.

We all have to grow up someday, though. Someday, you have to decide what kind of person you're going to be. Is faith going to be important in your life or are you just going to coast? You won't be any less beloved of God if you coast. You'll just have a different life.

It may be, also, that the end of life will loom threateningly in your imagination. It may be that you won't want to think about death, won't want to talk about it. Maybe you'll avoid making good healthcare decisions, maybe you won't make a will—too depressing. Because you haven't given much thought to what comes next. You're afraid to go there. *Don't remind me*, you tell your colleague who expresses incredulity at your refusal to plan.

Don't be afraid to follow. All those miracles in the Bible were signs of something beyond your life here, and they were written down so we might begin to come to terms with that in this world. Begin living as if it were true now. Begin trusting that it is.

WEDNESDAY IN EPIPHANY VIII

Pss 119:1–24 * 12, 13, 14
Proverbs 17:1–20
2 Timothy 3:1–17
John 13:1–20

"Lord, are you going to wash my feet?"
JOHN 13:6

My mother grew up in Duluth, so skating was a daily activity from autumn until well into March. Every day after school they would go home for their skates and head for the ice.

It was nearing suppertime one day, and it was time to go home. She would go to the warming house on the lake and get warm, then start back. But everyone else had the same idea: The warming house was packed. She would have had to ask someone to make room for her. And my mother was shy. She was afraid to ask. She would just walk home, she thought.

It was farther than she thought. The afternoon grew darker and darker, and the temperature began to drop. Her toes began to sting, and her walk grew clumsy. Then her feet grew numb, and it was even harder. She began to be afraid: cold, numb, far from home. She began to cry, and her tears froze on her cheeks. Then she stopped walking and sat down on the side of the road. So cold that she was confused. So cold that she was starting not to feel cold any more. She thought that she would probably die sitting there by the side of the road.

Her father came out looking for her. He picked her up and carried her home. He unlaced her boots in the kitchen and took them off, then removed her two pairs of wool socks. He brought snow in from the yard and rubbed her feet with it first, then switched to lukewarm water. Then warm water. Her feet hurt so badly she cried again. That was good, he said. The blood was coming back into them.

He saved her life. And then he washed her feet and saved them, too. The whole little package of her, saved by a father's love. No task is too small or too menial for love to enter and transform.

THURSDAY IN EPIPHANY VIII

Pss 18:1–20 * 18:21–50
Proverbs 21:30–22:6
2 Timothy 4:1–8
John 13:21–30

"Do quickly what you are going to do."
JOHN 13:27

We see the paradoxical relationship between God and evil elsewhere in scripture: in the book of Job, for instance, where it is with God's permission that Satan tempts poor Job with such terrible suffering, or when Jesus is tempted in the wilderness by a devil who is able to transport him bodily against his will. Or when he casts out a group of demons, who know him by name and bargain with him to cast them into a herd of pigs. Jesus knows evil. He isn't frightened by it. He names it for what it is, and it cannot triumph over him.

So his Passion and death are voluntary. He knows it's coming and submits to it. He knows Judas's intention and urges him to go on and get it over with.

Don't focus so much on the paradox that you miss the love. The whole point of a paradox is that our minds fail us when we try to understand it. It marries two things that ordinarily cannot speak to each other at all, and this paradox is no exception: good submitting willingly to evil. Nothing in the Passion it makes sense until we consider the love that motivates it.

Evil exists from the beginning, but its reality never cancels out the good. Its victories, devastating as they are, are temporary, and the good is stubbornly present alongside all of them, although it can be hard to find and often shows only much later. Why must it be so, we ask, if we are so beloved? Couldn't we just do without the evil altogether, live again in the Paradise of our first parents?

Why? I think the instances of God allowing evil we find in scripture are the writers' struggles with the fact that we cannot know where bad things come from, why we have them. We don't know. All we can know is what we decide to know: that life is so hard, but God is so good.

FRIDAY IN EPIPHANY VIII

Pss 16, 17 * 22
Proverbs 23:19–21, 29–24:2
2 Timothy 4:9–22
John 13:31–38

". . . before the cock crows, you will have denied me three times."
JOHN 13:38

We do not remember the times we have given in to weakness nearly as well as we cherish the memory of the times we have stood firm, but poor old Peter was never allowed to forget his moment of betrayal: It was recorded, and it survives him by two thousand years. We have lots of dirt on Peter, in fact: Every dumb thing he ever did was faithfully written down, almost as if someone were trying to make him look bad. Which is most interesting, since it is Peter who emerges into subsequent history as the head of the

Church—it makes me think Peter's *faux pas* must all be real, else why would they have been included at all?

His bumbling wrongheadedness always comforts me: Peter has the keys to the Kingdom, and even *he* doesn't get it right every time. He is impulsive. He is not brave. And then he is a new man: no longer hiding, no longer afraid, no longer denying anything, the new Peter knows what to do and he does it. After the resurrection, he becomes the leader through whom we inherit leadership in the church—this same foolish man. And in death, he joins his Lord: His life is taken from him by violence, and he is brave enough to face it.

Not always a hundred percent yourself? Have your bad days, too? Done a few things you regret? Me, too. Take heart, remember Peter, where he started and where he ended up, and have a fine day.

SATURDAY IN EPIPHANY VIII

Pss 20, 21:1–7 (8–14) * 110:1–5 (6–7), 116, 117
Proverbs 25:15–28
Philippians 1:1–11
John 18:1–14

And this is my prayer, that your love may overflow
more and more with knowledge and full insight
to help you to determine what is best. . . .
PHILIPPIANS 1:9–10

We'll be worshiping in the gym, not in the chapel, the conference director told me. *Okay.* I was in charge of worship for this one. I found the gym and went inside.

It was a college gymnasium: large, dark. Painted cinderblock walls. Basketball courts marked out on the floor. Fluorescent lighting. *Okay.*

I grabbed the piano cover off the baby grand and draped it over a chair, and then I propped the icon up with three prayer books behind it and placed two candles in front of it. It looked like a chair with an icon sitting on it. The two candles looked like headlights.

I guess it's a gym, no matter what you do, I thought, standing behind the back row of chairs to get a long-distance view of the icon.

Let's try this box, someone said, and we installed a large box on the chair. We propped up the icon with prayer books, and added more candles, candles in twos and threes, candles in holders and candles in bottles, candles in goblets.

It was still a gym.

The light was all wrong. We propped open the outside doors and began flipping circuit breakers, losing bank after bank of dead-looking fluorescent lights. Now indirect light from the fading day filtered into the room, and the candles made golden pools of light around themselves. Better. Not excellent, not up to my standard, but better.

We used the rite for Night Prayer from the New Zealand Prayer Book. *Lord, it is night. The night is for stillness. Let us be still in the presence of God. It is night after a long day. What has been done has been done; what has not been done has not been done; let it be.*

It was still a gym.

Let it be.

SUNDAY, LAST EPIPHANY

Pss 148, 149, 150 * 114, 115
Ecclesiasticus 48:1–11
2 Corinthians 3:7–18
Luke 9:18–27

"But truly I tell you, there are some standing here who will not taste death before they see the kingdom of God."
LUKE 9:27

The plane bumps and plunges along, like a sled on an uneven hill. It is hard not to be afraid; every time I encounter turbulence on a flight, I wonder why I came. Why I didn't say no, what it would mean if I were to die on my way to wherever I am going. The sickening downward spiral, the flying pocketbooks and magazines, the sudden release of all the oxygen masks at the same time, popping down before our terrified eyes and whipping around crazily as we hurtled toward the ground. I would not survive. None of us would.

Once in a while, though, a baby does. They find her, still strapped in her seat, wailing lustily. Why is that, I wonder? Their little bodies are softer and weaker than ours. They don't know enough to put on a life jacket or a mask. But sometimes a baby lives, when all the adults have perished.

I wonder if it has something to do with not being afraid. With not bracing oneself against tragedy, using that energy to live, instead. I wonder if the moment-to-moment way babies live protects them sometimes. Only sometimes, of course; more of them would survive disasters if it were always true. But it is an appealing thought, that our fear might be what hurts us most of all.

When I fly with Q, I find his hand when we hit a rough spot. Sometimes I look into his eyes. He never looks to be afraid. I can see that he knows I am, though. Neither of us speaks. There is nothing unsaid between us, nothing that needs saying.

Then I, too, am not afraid. I remember that the ordeal of dying does not go on forever, that dying itself is quick, that dying in this way would probably be over in an instant. That the love which comforts me, human love from a human being, is only a small token of all the love there is. We swim in the love of God as a fish swims in water, fly in it as a bird flies in the air. We breathe it, forever.

MONDAY IN LAST EPIPHANY

Pss 25 * 9, 15
Proverbs 27:1–6, 10–12
Philippians 2:1–13
John 18:15–18, 25–27

Do not boast about tomorrow,
for you do not know what a day may bring.
PROVERBS 27:1

et's wait until next year . . . One of these days, I'm going to write a
book . . . Learn Greek . . . Take a drawing class . . . When I retire,
I'm going to travel . . . in a couple of years . . . maybe later . . . someday.

No—now. As much as possible, now. Tomorrow is not promised us. The life you have had may, at any moment, become all the life you're going to get in this world.

Still—and probably for the rest of my career—I encounter survivors of the World Trade Center bombing at the retreats I lead throughout the country. I meet them in other states, but I meet them especially here, in New York or Connecticut or New Jersey.

I was in the building across the street, in a meeting. We heard the noise of the first collapse but we didn't know what it was. I didn't go to the window, but a lot of people did. So I didn't see the people jump. I couldn't look . . . I was on the thirtieth floor and I just started walking because I remembered the last time in '93 and all I knew was that I was going to get out of there . . . My wife couldn't get through to me until afternoon. I was going crazy at home . . . I looked up and saw the first plane hit . . . I saw a plane flying low right along the length of Manhattan and I thought to myself, why is it flying so low? . . . We were all on our rooftops, watching from the East Village, every building had people on the roof, and when we saw the first tower go down everyone just screamed. Yeah, just screams, going up from all the rooftops . . .

A day like any day. Every last day is a day like any day, with one important difference: There aren't any more after it. It was the last one. You don't know until afterward. And then, of course, you're not here anymore.

After everything is over here, after that last day, we affirm that life continues in Christ. It is not historical life—history happens only here. But it is a life for which we can prepare, so that our leaving of this one for its mysterious glory need not be a remorseful moment of bitter might-have-beens. Short and uncertain, this life is nonetheless lovely, as lovely as we are willing to make it. Lovelier still, in fact, for its very uncertainty: You don't have all the time in the world in which to find its meaning and beauty, don't have forever to find a way to be kind and learn the peculiar joy of kindness.

TUESDAY IN LAST EPIPHANY

Pss 26, 28 * 36, 39
Proverbs 30:1–4, 24–33
Philippians 3:1–11
John 18:28–38

Surely I am too stupid to be human. . . .
PROVERBS 30:2

It's one of those days: I've already exceeded my quota of errors and it's not even noon yet. Stupid little things: paid the same bill twice and another one not at all, gone all the way to the store with a list and still managed to omit the milk that was the main thing we needed. Waited way too long to return a phone call, succumbing childishly to the irrational fear of telephoning I really ought to have outgrown by now. Maybe I should just cancel this afternoon and go to bed, where I can't do any more damage. Start again tomorrow.

Actually, that's not such a bad idea. Sometimes we crash, like our computers, and all we can do is shut down and restart. Begin again, on a new path, for we have lots of different paths from which to choose. But it doesn't mean we're "too stupid to be human" when this happens: I recognize my own harsh self-criticism in the ancient voice of this writer, but he's not right about himself, and neither am I. We aren't less human when we make mistakes; we are more so. Being human means we're not perfect. Not going to become perfect, not today and not ever.

But if I accept my imperfections, aren't I just giving up? It can't be right to accept things that are wrong, can it?

But accepting reality isn't the same as approving it. Our mistakes are still errors, our sins still sins. I don't know how to come out on the other side of them, without somehow calling a truce for now so we can make a fresh start. If I remain impaled on all of my faults, all I can do is continue to bewail them. Enough already. One apology does it. Now it's time to do what it takes to get moving again.

Back to the store for the forgotten milk. Write out that missing check and mail it. Maybe a nap, or at least a nice bubble bath to clear the mind and comfort the body. And then, tomorrow is another day.

Lent

ASH WEDNESDAY

Pss 95, 32, 143 * 102, 130
Amos 5:6–15
Hebrews 12:1–14
Luke 18:9–14

*". . . for all who exalt themselves will be humbled,
but all who humble themselves will be exalted."*
LUKE 18:14

How are you feeling these days? someone asks, and I say that I am fine. And I *am* fine: All the electrical systems in my heart work like a clock now, all its plumbing is repaired. I am back at the gym, working up a welcome sweat, managing to produce a pulse in three digits for the first time in many months.

And yet a certain *disarray* continues. My memory is so poor that it cannot even be said to play tricks on me: It's not smart enough to play a trick. Important engagements slide off the slick surface of my mind—I can almost see them disappear, even as I reach for them, see the terrible grey sheen of a slickness that shouldn't be there. Shouldn't my brain be more—eventful? Shouldn't things stick in its folds? Nothing sticks.

And so, while sins of commission are down, sins of omission are definitely up: I have not done those things that I ought to have done. The prayer book used to add, after that line in the general confession, *And there is no health in us*, but we dropped it in 1979. It seemed to lack the cheeriness upon which we insisted in those days—remember that the 70s were the decade that brought us the smiley face.

I miss *And there is no health in us*. Not because I romanticize illness—use a few bedpans and the glamour is plumb gone. But I have learned that my health and my goodness and even my mind are not *in* me. These things may be part of me, but they are all gifts: Though I may husband my health, I don't *make* it. Don't create it. Don't set its limits. Its comings and goings remain mysterious. The miracle of the human body and mind and conscience, their faithful housing and holding of life, their brave struggles to remain whole, to regain lost ground—these are imagined and then given by One more wonderful, even, than all their intricacies.

Thanks and thanks and thanks be to God. Let my disarray only show me what wonders I had, what wonders God still imagines. Still gives.

THURSDAY AFTER
ASH WEDNESDAY

Pss 37:1–18 * 37:19–42
Habakkuk 3:1–10 (11–15) 16–18
Philippians 3:12–21
John 17:1–8

*I glorified you on earth by finishing
the work that you gave me to do.*
JOHN 17:4

I knelt beside the open coffin to pray. Bob wore his firefighter's dress blues, which was no surprise—he loved the firehouse, which was right down the street from his house, and he had been with the company for decades. He was chief in the early 80s, and so his uniform bore his chief's ribbons, and the hat next to him bore that title: "Chief." A firefighter stood at silent attention nearby, keeping watch.

There really isn't a figure in our society more Christlike than a volunteer firefighter. No less vulnerable to sudden tragedy than any other citizen, they choose to handle their vulnerability differently: face into it, sacrifice it, if need be, to the well-being of their fellow citizens. Someone has to do this, if the community is to go on. But most people don't. Only a few.

His grandchildren were inconsolable—he was a loving grandfather, demonstrative, open to their emotions and to his own. I remember when his kids were young—they took up a whole pew in those days, scrubbed and combed for Sunday morning. They are middle-aged, now, incredibly—it's one of the consistent amazements of ministry in churches, the way children become adults, while you don't feel any older yourself. Now, with their mother and their own children, it was more like four pews of Hallbauers.

Bob could never understand how a person could live in the world and just decide not to help other people. How a person could live a self-absorbed life. *I just don't see how they can do that*, he said over and over, as he lay there so ill, not completely in his right mind. Part of that refrain was code: He was saying that he couldn't understand what was happening to his body, why he could no longer seem to be himself. But part of it really was a reflection on how he had lived his life, a cry of mourning for a world in which too few people elect to live theirs that way.

But a person can change that overnight. We can decide to be another way, and it is never too late to make that choice. What will the world lose when it loses you? What will you leave it? The grandchildren wept in their seats, and wept again at the burial, when the honor guard from the United States Army folded the flag and presented it to their grandma, when "Taps" was played. But they have each been left a gift: They had a chance to know a man whose example was a sterling one. They have seen firsthand what a father can be, and a citizen.

Don't ever forget who he was, I told them in the sermon, *and tell the little ones who won't remember today. Make sure they know.* And they looked at me through their tears, a little surprised that I was talking right to them. But of course I was: They were the most important people there. They are the ones who own the future—we all belong to the past. If Bob's example lives on, it will be because they have carried it with them. *Don't ever forget*, I told them again.

FRIDAY AFTER
ASH WEDNESDAY

Pss 95, 31 * 35
Ezekiel 18:1–4, 25–32
Philippians 4:1–19
John 17:9–19

Do not worry about anything. . . .
PHILIPPIANS 4:6

Such a gentle plane ride home. Such a nice walk from the train. So good to be back in our own house, our own bed. So good to see Q.
Everybody was asking after you, I told him.
No, they weren't.
Yes, they really were. You're famous, you know. There was a sound of a little bell and then the sudden soft pounce of cat feet on the quilt. *But Noodle is more famous, I'm afraid. More people asked after her than you.*

Noodle walked carefully up one of Q's legs until she had reached his chest and was higher than either of us, which is always her goal. She stared down at Q, who began to rub her neck. With a half-hearted nip at his fingers for old time's sake, she settled down into a comfortable crouch and began her purr.

Noodle is still working on her purr. Each cat has his own, of course: Kate's purr was bigger than she was. Nobody has ever gotten close to What's-Her-Name to hear hers. I have heard tigers and lions purring at the zoo, a sound like the engine of a small airplane.

We think cats' purring means they're happy, but Kate was purring right up until the moment she died: There she was, on the steel examining table, so unwell, so bony and so small. She can't have been happy. But we were cuddling and stroking her, putting our faces down into her beautiful fur, telling her what a fine cat she was, and she purred and purred.

So maybe she was happy. Even though she was dying. Maybe she had a sense of completeness in her life, and maybe she was tired and knew that now she could rest. Maybe she liked feeling the same loving hands she'd felt her whole life, stroking her as she left it. Maybe that was just all right.

Perhaps her contentment came from within, after all, not from circumstance. Perhaps memory was a big part of it, a bringing forward of the good times she had lived. Perhaps our happiness can be like that, too: *retroactive*. Our sorrows certainly are: We drag *them* around with us through a lifetime and don't even know it. But perhaps our blessings can stay with us, too, return in imagination and memory to bless us again. Perhaps we have some kind of a purr within when we take them out and study them, marveling again at our good fortune in ever having had them at all.

SATURDAY AFTER ASH WEDNESDAY

Pss 30, 32 * 42, 43
Ezekiel 39:21–29
Philippians 4:10–20
John 17:20–26

I know what it is to have little,
and I know what it is to have plenty.
PHILIPPIANS 4:12

It's more than thirty years ago now, and I haven't thought about it in ages. My baby didn't know we were poor, but I sure did: It was a terrible January day, down in the teens, and we were making the trip home from the doctor's office by bus. She was bundled in her stroller, a rickety affair that I had gotten with S&H Green Stamps. They didn't have those clear plastic enclosures to keep out the cold on infant strollers in those days, and the icy wind cut right through just about anything you had on. We huddled at the bus stop, I crouching down beside her, encircling her with my arms in attempt to put myself between her and the bitter cold.

The bus was late. It didn't come and then it didn't come some more. The wind blew air that seemed to be getting even colder as we huddled there. I fought back tears: they wouldn't do any good, might freeze my eyes shut and might scare my baby, who seemed to be doing all right surrounded by her mother, her secondhand snow-suit and all those blankets.

Then a truck pulled up and its passenger door opened. *It's too damn cold to be out here with a baby,* a rough voice said. *Where are you going?*

Back to College Park, I said. Never accept rides from strangers, I said to myself. You don't know this person.

Get in, he ordered. I looked at his face, looked at my baby, looked again in vain for the bus, swallowed hard and climbed in. He got out and folded up the stroller, settling it in the cab behind my seat. It was blessedly warm inside.

Sure is cold, I said. *I'm grateful to you for stopping. I don't know where the bus is today.*

It's too cold for you to be out there with the baby.

I know, I said. He was right. *I'd like to pay you a little something for gas.*

Naw. Where shall I drop you?

Well, the store would be fine, thank you. I had a little more than two dollars in my purse: thirty cents for the bus and two dollars for food. That's not enough for much of anything today, but in those days you could feed a family on twenty dollars a week, and I could do it on ten.

I don't remember what we talked about as we drove along—it wasn't far. I would buy some groceries in the warmth of the grocery store and then Corinna and I could easily make the ten blocks home on foot. Besides, my benefactor was just rough enough that I didn't want him to see where I lived.

But he was kind. Kind to me—unfolded the stroller onto the sidewalk in front of the store. Just as I left the warmth of the cab, I sneaked the thirty cents I would have spent on the bus onto his dashboard. *Thanks,* I said. *It was nice of you to stop for us.*

I was in the canned goods aisle of the store when he reappeared, looking fierce. I started when I saw him—what was he doing here?

He picked up my hand and thrust the thirty cents into it. *I could kill you for doing that*, he said, and turned around and left before I could even respond.

I stood there with the coins in my hand. My good Samaritan, though not as poor as I was, was not a rich man, either. I had sought to deny him the joy of doing a kindness with no expectation of return and he, in his rough way, had corrected me. Even the poor are ennobled and delighted by giving.

I finished our meager shopping and pushed the stroller home. The wind wasn't as biting now, and the walk was outwardly uneventful. I thought of him, though, my angry good Samaritan, the whole way.

SUNDAY, LENT I

Pss 63:1–8 (9–11), 98 * 103
Daniel 9:3–10
Hebrews 2:10–18
John 12:44–50

*For the one who sanctifies and those who
are sanctified all have one Father.*
HEBREWS 2:11

Dreams, lately, of the humiliating, shaming kind: I am in a public place and find to my horror that I have neglected to wear a skirt. I open my mouth to speak before a crowd of people and find that I am mute. The people who invited me are angry; the audience grows impatient—finally I slink off the stage in utter defeat, attempting to explain to someone, anyone, but unable to speak.

You mustn't blow your own horn. Don't talk about what you do well. Don't admit to doing anything well. Be modest and self-effacing. It's very wrong to be proud of yourself.

And something bad will happen if you are. Like forgetting to wear your skirt. Or losing your voice. Is there someone, somewhere who has not known the struggle between the sense of giftedness and the reality of falling short? Someone who has not longed for credit where credit is due, and then felt ashamed of that longing? Where does honest delight in accomplishment end and pride begin?

The truth is, it is not just those who exalt themselves who will be humbled: We will all be humbled. None of us are getting out of here alive, and the dying are not ordinarily the picture of health and strength: We all have some tough times ahead. This passage may be much less about cultivating a neurotic reluctance to commend the good that is in us than it is about the mortality we all share.

We will all fall, but those who refuse to humble themselves beforehand will fall farther. Those for whom any sort of self-denial is an outrage are certain to be outraged by what is certain to happen to them one day. Those unaccustomed to doing without will suffer more; they won't be used to it. Now is the time to cultivate resources other than those upon which the world depends, resources within ourselves, things that cannot be taken from us when everything else has been.

Those who have nothing else continue to have the love of God. Those who have much have the love of God, too. Rummage among your many possessions now, and find it in an unexpected place within you, against the time when you, too, have only that love to sustain you.

MONDAY IN LENT I

Pss 41, 52 * 44
Genesis 37:1–11
1 Corinthians 1:1–19
Mark 1:1–13

And just as he was coming up out of the water, he saw the heavens torn apart and the Spirit descending like a dove on him.
MARK 1:10

Q says the carpet in our bedroom, which belonged to his parents, is from Iran and dates from 1917—it has its Islamic date on its center medallion, most unusual in an oriental. At least, Q tells me that's the date. I've always suspected that it really says "Yankee Go Home," but who knows?

But whatever—it's not a rug Noodle should be sharpening her claws on in the middle of the night. *Noodle!* we shout in unison from the bed, and the scratching pauses for a moment and then resumes. *Noodle!* Q says, again, sharply. Nothing. I try a gentler soprano *Noodle!* She scratches the carpet in answer.

I get up and find the catnip, which we keep in Q's underwear drawer for just such emergencies. I sprinkle some on the pad of cheap carpet we keep especially for Noodle to scratch on, and she succumbs to its allure, lying down on the little rectangle, arching her back and rubbing the back of her head in the catnip. You can count on catnip to hypnotize a cat for a good half-hour, and then after that maybe she'll move on to something else.

Cats are good smellers. Gypsy comes down from the third floor to see what smells so nice, and heads for the little rectangle. That carpet isn't big enough for both of them, so I forestall a catfrontation by getting up again to put more catnip on the base of the little spring toy that they're supposed to bat back and forth and enjoy. Gypsy winds her considerable bulk around it and begins to writhe in delight. I don't recall any substance ever making me feel that good, and I came of age in the 1960s. I think it would distrust it instinctively if it did. We're just not supposed to be that ecstatic.

People in the Bible were, though, and frequently. When the spirit descended upon somebody in the Old Testament, you knew it: They fell down on the ground and didn't come back to themselves for ages. Some of them were accused of being drunk. The disciples, too, seemed drunk to at least one of their early audiences, before they figured out how to curb their enthusiasm just a little. The people of the early church spoke in tongues when the spirit fell on them; people in Pentecostal communities still do.

Many Episcopal worship services impress visitors as being awfully quiet affairs. A long period of silence after a reading makes a newcomer wonder if the officiant has gone home, or died, or lost his place in his prayer book. The prayer is quiet, and the rush of names in the free intercessions are quiet, too, and in some places there are none. Nobody answers back the preacher or encourages her with a shouted "Amen!" or "Yes, it is!" To some visitors, all this quite seems sad. *Couldn't we be little more, well, joyful?* one of them might ask.

I suppose each of has a brand of joy that suits us. Perhaps we have several: some loud and some quiet. Some joy laughs and some joy smiles almost imperceptibly. Some joy throws its arms around its neighbor in a big bear hug and other joy offers a warm hand-shake or even a wordless smile and wave from across a crowded church. We are who we are. We love who and what we love, and we do it in the ways that come naturally.

TUESDAY IN LENT I

Pss 45 * 47, 48
Genesis 37:12–24
1 Corinthians 1:20–31
Mark 1:14–28

God chose what is weak in the world to shame the strong. . . .
1 CORINTHIANS 1:27

What happen here? the manicurist will ask me today, I know—I have a deep puncture in the cuticle of my right thumb. I know less Korean than she does English, so it will be challenging to explain that I picked up a twenty-two-pound cat with one hand securely under her chest and a full cup of tea in the other hand and that the cat didn't like it and twisted out of my grasp and because I didn't have a convenient spot on which to set down my tea, the cat ended up suspended by one claw from the cuticle of my right thumb. She didn't like that, either—let out a yell you don't often hear from a cat. I don't know which of us found the experience more painful. I hope it was the cat. Serves her right if it was.

What happened? And how quickly did it happen? And how dumb was it—accidents are always a split second of being in the wrong place at the wrong time. Just an inch in the other direction, just a second earlier, and you wouldn't be in this fix. *If only I'd taken the other route home, stopped to get the mail first, checked the position of the knob on the stove.*

But what's done is done. An accident plunges you into a new reality, sometimes with a new and permanent set of parameters within which you must attempt to do whatever it is that you wanted to do. Sometimes it robs you of the possibility of doing it at all, and you have to do something else instead. The flexible courage and strength of people who have had to make this adjustment in life are breathtaking. We look at them in their wheelchairs, at their crutches, their white canes, their asymmetrical gaits, and we think we are seeing weakness.

No. Not weakness. Not at all. What we are seeing is strength, beyond what most of us can even imagine.

WEDNESDAY IN LENT I

Pss 119:49–72 * 49, (53)
Genesis 37:25–36
1 Corinthians 2:1–13
Mark 1:29–45

In the morning, while it was still very dark, he got up and went out to a deserted place, and there he prayed. And Simon and his companions hunted for him. When they found him, they said to him, "Everyone is searching for you."

MARK 1:35–37

There was simply no letup: first Simon's mother-in-law, then dozens, scores, *hundreds* of the sick—"the whole city," Mark says. And the next day, Jesus got up really, really early—"A great while before day"—and slipped out of Simon's house without telling anybody. He needed some quiet.

But it was not to be. They came after him and found him. There was more to do. Not here, though—they set off down the road to the next town. I suppose he could have spent weeks in that town and not run out of people to heal. He had to leave, even though there was more left to do. I wonder if that was hard for him.

He has a wise rhythm: work and rest. He makes times for prayer and it is part of his rest to pray. It fills him up. He needed this rhythm: he may have been truly God, but he was also truly human. He got tired.

I have been a person who took a perverse pride in my exhaustion. Wore it like a badge of honor. I have been proud of being a hard worker, and I almost worked myself to death as a direct result of that pride. I still feel guilty, sometimes, when I see someone else working as hard as I used to work. *I should be doing that*, I think.

And it *is* good to be a hard worker. Jesus was one. But he had the sense to rest and refuel. I need to have that sense, too. And so do you, even if something more anxious is what comes naturally to us. Because we are not more powerful than he.

THURSDAY IN LENT I

Pss 50 * (59, 60) or 19, 46
Genesis 39:1–23
1 Corinthians 2:14–3:15
Mark 2:1–12

*The chief jailer paid no heed to anything that was
in Joseph's care, because the Lord was with him;
and whatever he did, the Lord made it prosper.*
GENESIS 39:23

I wish I had someone like Joseph around—he is the perfect administrator, and everyone who comes into contact with him sees it immediately, even his jailer. If Joseph worked for me, my life would hum along so smoothly I wouldn't recognize it as my life.

Administration is a spiritual gift not often recognized as such. Prophecy, preaching, prayer—sure, we can tell those are spiritual. But the spiritual life is lived in the context of ordinary human life:

Somebody has to order the candles and the altar bread. Somebody has to pay the bills. Somebody has to make things run.

Joseph is that rare bird who combines both kinds of spiritual gifts: He is also the dreamer, the one who interprets dreams. And he is a person who gets things done. He is a whole person. He would have made a good parish priest, but parishes and priests were several thousand years into the future.

Not many of us are as well-rounded as Joseph is—we tend to be a little lopsided. By the time we're grown, most of us have figured out where we shine. And what we're better off delegating. Nothing is sadder than watching someone struggling to stay in a position for which he has not been given the needed gifts, unless it's being in that place yourself.

Better to go, as soon as possible, and get to the place for which God *has* equipped you.

FRIDAY IN LENT I

Pss 95, 40, 54 * 51
Genesis 40:1–23
1 Corinthians 3:16–23
Mark 2:13–22

*Do you not know that you are God's temple
and that God's spirit dwells in you?*
1 CORINTHIANS 3:16

The fluorescent lights in the train are bright, and outside it is dark. But both the train and the night outside belong to God.

I can see my reflection in the window. My shawl came from the thrift shop a few years ago: I was the rector of the church, and I usually got a chance to buy things as soon as they were unpacked. My favorite black loafers are on their second replacement soles. Old things, but they've still got a lot of wear left in them. And both belong to Christ.

When I turn sideways and look at myself in the mirror, there is a bulge in my middle which I would prefer not to see. I can suck it in, and then I look pretty good. But my whole lumpy body belongs to Christ.

We are almost in Penn Station, have almost reached my beloved city. Loud and crowded, vulgar and glorious: the whole of New York City is Christ's. He is so loving that the fact that many, if not most, New Yorkers don't think about him much or follow other faiths altogether doesn't trouble him at all. He loves them all just the same.

We are so imperfect, all of us. Everything and everyone here, so flawed and yet so beloved. Some of us are most concerned to conceal our blemishes from one another, and some of us even hope to conceal them from God, a doomed enterprise if ever there was one. But we really needn't worry. We are beloved anyway, whoever and whatever we are, however smoothly—or not—we live our lives.

SATURDAY IN LENT I

Pss 55 * 138, 139:1–17 (18–23)
Genesis 41:1–13
1 Corinthians 4:1–7
Mark 2:23–3:6

But with me it is a very small thing that I should be judged by you or by any human court.
1 CORINTHIANS 4:3

Sometimes people radically overvalue the devotion of the clergy, and sometimes they profoundly undervalue it. If they love you anyway, your simple good morning is greeted as if it were the song of angels. And, if they're having second thoughts about you, you just can't please them. You matter a great deal to your congregation, more than you're worth, really: You symbolize all their dreams of what church ought to be, and some of those dreams are just that—dreams.

Sometimes weary clergy succumb to a bitter feeling: I work myself to death around here, and it's never good enough. Someone always has a complaint. I don't make a lot of money. I don't have enough time for my family. Why did I ever choose this life?

The fact is, of course, that it is they who are the heroes of the church, not you. They are the ones who give unstintingly, who come in to a meeting after a long day at work, who come over on a Saturday morning to do yard work. It is your job to be here, to preach well, to be faithful in visiting the sick. To the best of the church's ability, you get paid for being here. They're all volunteers, there only because they think it important to be there.

And the other fact is that you *didn't* choose it. It chose you. You were *called* to this life. You would not be who you are if you were *not* doing this. The absence of calling is readily apparent in someone who is serving out a misplaced ministry against the weight of his gifts and talents, but the presence of calling sustains even the most draining ministries beyond what any of us have the right to expect.

Sometimes a failure of physical or mental health ends service in a particular place before you would have it end. That happened to me, and it was painful. But it didn't end my call to preach: It only altered the form of it.

Live according to your calling, lay or ordained, and your work is a stream of living water, strong enough to undergo many changes in form, if that is God's desire.

SUNDAY, LENT II

Pss 24, 29 * 8, 84
Genesis 41:14–45
Romans 6:3–14
John 5:19–24

". . . there is none so discreet and wise as you.
You shall be over my house, and all my people
shall order themselves as you command. . . ."
GENESIS 41:39–40

Let someone be proposed for public office and an immediate fact-finding frenzy begins: Did he smoke marijuana in the 60s? Did he have an affair? Cheat on his taxes? Hire an undocumented worker? Many an appointment has run aground on these rocks, leaving us to search for leadership among the negatively qualified: people who haven't done things.

And yet certain leaders have survived fairly convincing public airing of their own sin and remained in power, forcing the public to wrestle painfully with the manner in which personal sin and virtue coexist with civic leadership. How good do we need our leaders to be?

The Bible is interestingly frank on this score: It gives us some glimpses into the seamy side of figures we admire. David, for instance, from whose lineage the Savior comes, is an adulterer and contracts out a murder—the writer didn't have to share this with us, but he did. St. Paul was a persecutor of Christians and colluded in the murder of at least one. Nobody tries very hard to clean up these biographies. They present our leaders to us as they were, warts and all.

God can work with us even if we have done things we ought not to have done. Everybody has. The important thing about these things is that we understand now that they are wrong and hurtful to ourselves or to others or to both, whatever we may have told ourselves at the time. And what we learned—the hard way—from having done them.

MONDAY IN LENT II

Pss 56, 57, (58) * 64, 65
Genesis 41:46–57
1 Corinthians 4:8–20 (21)
Mark 3:7–19a

Already you have all you want!
Already you have become rich!
1 CORINTHIANS 4:8

At the time, it seems that the wedding inaugurates a happily-ever-after eternity of uneventful bliss, but the signs of some-thing more complicated are already there at the reception: the introvert hiding from the extravert, the in-laws rolling their eyes at the vulgarity of what the bride has chosen for the menu, for the color scheme, the cake. Two exhausted young people, happy to hide, at last, from both their families as they slide the bolt shut on their hotel room door. Neither says anything, but the thought crosses both their minds: Life together may not always be easy.

But most people want life together with someone dear anyway. At first they don't believe in the hard parts at all, but even later on, when they cannot help but believe in them, their hearts have inter-twined and it would be hard to pull them apart. A thousand stories, a satchel full of private jokes, dozens of code words incomprehensi-ble to anyone but them. And when the time comes for one to leave, the one remaining realizes that she has lost a part of her self.

Was it worth all the trouble? Is the pain of the ending so great you'd rather never have gone there to begin with? St. Paul thought so—not so much because of the pain of parting, but because he couldn't imagine that the normal day-to-day obligations and annoyances could possibly be worth it.

But of cource, he never tried it. Paul had the gift of celibacy, I guess: the power to be productively alone. Besides, he could be cranky: Some first-century Jewish woman should have thanked her lucky stars that he converted before her family had a chance to marry her off to him.

But of course, she didn't know about any of that. She just wanted to get married.

TUESDAY IN LENT II

Pss 61, 62 * 68:1–20 (21–23) 24–36
Genesis 42:1–17
1 Corinthians 5:1–8
Mark 3:19b–35

"Who are my mother and my brothers?"
MARK 3:33

In an odd way, this is a reassuring story: Jesus' family didn't understand *him*, either. The struggle to break free of the people who loved him most was hard for Jesus, as it is for us. It makes sense that this is so: The people who love you have dreams and desires for you. They want you to be all right. At least one of them wants this more than she wants anything else in the world.

The tug-of-war is painful for us and it was painful for him. We often make second families, of friends and neighbors, people *we* have chosen. Jesus did that, too. It seemed to him that these relationships were more intimate than the ones he had with relatives, and this hurt and frightened his family.

He does not obey his mother and brothers when they come to bring him home. Some decisions in life are too important to be left to anyone else, even family members who love you. There are things in life you must decide for yourself, and your relationship with God is one of them. No matter how much they love you, your family can't do that for you. It is yours to handle.

We know, of course, where Jesus' mother ended up: She went to live with his best friend after he died. She made the journey from this pathetic and doomed attempt to rein him in to the very foot of the cross. She was able to follow him there when others were not.

The old love and the new love united, as Jesus fulfilled his mission in the world. His mother and his friends helped him do it, each out of a love uniquely his, uniquely hers. Like all loves. No one else can love for us. We must love—God and everything else—for ourselves.

WEDNESDAY IN LENT II

Pss 72 * 119:73–96
Genesis 42:18–28
1 Corinthians 5:9–6:8
Mark 4:1–20

"Listen! A sower went out to sow."
MARK 4:3

It was ages ago, back in the early fall when I was clearing out more ivy to enlarge a flower bed or two out front. It was inevitable that some buried tulip bulbs would come up with the ivy, and they did. I'll put them back in when I finish, I thought, and made a neatish pile on the sidewalk. But someone was coming for an appointment or I needed to catch a train: I scooped up all the bulbs and put them in a dish. I'll just leave it here on the windowsill where I'm sure to see it, and stick them in this weekend. Well, next weekend. *Soon.*

Outside, the ground froze. Inside, Thanksgiving came and went, and Christmas. Outside, ice and snow. Inside, dishes and baking, the clatter of plates in the dish drainer. Forgotten, the tulip bulbs sat in their dish in the window sill, withered brown husks, and watched it all. I didn't even get around to giving up on them.

And this morning I notice that they have sprouted. With no encouragement from me or anyone else, the brown husks have fallen away to reveal creamy living bulbs, pale green shoots of an inch or more emerging from their pointed tops. Quick: a saucer of pebbles, some water. They'll bloom. Tulips in the spring.

Well, it's never too late. You can't screw up so badly that God can't find something worth building in the wreckage, that life can't assert its return when it is time. Life can be dispiriting: It is running out, like sand through an hourglass. But it is also exciting: just look at what can happen sometimes! And you don't even have to put a nickel in!

THURSDAY IN LENT II

Pss (70), 71 * 74
Genesis 42:29–38
1 Corinthians 6:12–20
Mark 4:21–34

*Do you not know that whoever is united
to a prostitute becomes one body with her?*
1 CORINTHIANS 6:16

No, I don't think a prostitute's clients *do* know that, not usually. I think they understand the encounter to be of much shorter duration. An hour's fun. A victimless crime, it is often called. The oldest profession.

It's certainly true that it's been around forever. But that doesn't mean it's victimless. Or that it's a profession. Few people enter it by choice, and few find any joy in it beyond its remuneration.

Sooner, or later, loveless sex invades the rest of life, making it impossible to hold the sacrament of human love next to the heart. People don't know this is happening while they're doing it. They don't realize it until later.

Is there a remedy for the victims of this "victimless" crime? Are they soiled beyond cleansing, never to be restored to cleanness of body and spirit? Jesus' compassion for more than one such woman signals us that it is not so. An older and wiser chastity can replace the shopworn spirit. Perhaps we can't go home again, but we can have a different home. Men and women alike, those who know they have been soiled and those who do not—they can be redeemed and made new, fitted for a love that ennobles them or fitted to live alone with integrity in the light of a love that sees its own image in their newly cleansed souls.

There is probably no such thing as casual sex. Like it or not, we are joined with those with whom we are that intimate: In more ways than just the epidemiological, they leave their mark on us and we on them. Human society forests the sexual act with rules for a reason: It's dynamite, and needs to be handled with care. For our own good.

FRIDAY IN LENT II

Pss 95, 69:1–23 (24–30) 31–38 * 73
Genesis 43:1–15
1 Corinthians 7:1–9
Mark 4:35–41

"Why are you afraid? Have you still no faith?"
MARK 4:40

The disciples were experienced seafarers; they knew the difference between real trouble and a little rolling, and this was real trouble. They would not have wakened him if they had not been in mortal fear.

But they did awaken him. They did think he could do something to help them, and this is remarkable, because—unlike all of them—Jesus was not a seafarer at all. He was the son of a carpenter and, almost certainly, a carpenter by training himself. So it wasn't his maritime experience they called on. It must have been something else.

Jesus is teasing them. *What are you guys, scared? Aw, c'mon.* He knows they have faith in him or they would not be calling on him. He is not afraid, but he knows good and well they are. And yet their fear has not inhibited their faith, far from it: It has been a place to exercise it. Fear brings faith forward—if only because we have nothing else upon which to stand.

Afraid sometimes? Angry sometimes? Lonely and sad? Discouraged? The presence of fear or anger or sorrow in life doesn't mean our faith has gone missing. It means it's about to go to work, calling upon the Lord in desperation. At the end of our rope, in whatever situation brings us to the end of it, there is Jesus. Ready to begin where we leave off.

SATURDAY IN LENT II

Pss 75, 76 * 23, 27
Genesis 43:16–34
1 Corinthians 7:10–24
Mark 5:1–20

. . . for he had often been restrained with shackles
and chains, but the chains he wrenched apart,
and the shackles he broke in pieces. . . .
MARK 5:4

We know this about our own demons: They can't be subdued by force. They break out of their chains, or they sneak out of them. We can't cast out our own demons; if we could, they wouldn't possess us. We would be free.

Notice that the demons use the voice of the demoniac, as they use the rest of his body. They speak with his voice. That is why he is so much more fearsome than other sick people: He appears to be himself, but he doesn't act like himself. His voice is his voice, but it doesn't speak his words, but someone else's. Frightening.

Mental illness is this man's demon. Ours might not be as loud or violent, but they are demons nonetheless: things that have taken up residence within us to do us harm. Cigarettes, maybe, or a destructive relationship. Alcohol, of course—there was a reason why the nineteenth century called it "Demon Rum." Hurtful things can be so stubbornly present in us that it is not hard to see why the ancients thought of them as willful parasites with actual personalities. That's the way they act.

The demons in the New Testament must be cast out by someone who has authority over them, and Jesus has that authority. They may be bigger than we are, but he is bigger than they. Try your whole life to rid yourself of one of them and you may never succeed; call upon the power higher than your own power, and you have made a beginning.

SUNDAY, LENT III

Pss 93, 96 * 34
Genesis 44:1–17
Romans 8:1–10
John 5:25–29

"... the dead will hear the voice of the Son of God ..."
JOHN 5:25

It was a dream, of course: It was *now*, and I was all grown up, but somehow I was sleeping in my little-girl bed in our old house. It was morning: I could hear my father down in the kitchen, preparing our breakfast of tea and toast. Amid the occasional clatter of dishes, I could hear the low rumble of his voice as he sang a hymn to himself, something he did every morning. Not daring to believe my ears—my father has been dead for a long time—I put on my bathrobe and hurried downstairs.

There he was, just as always: wearing his old grey sweater, looking at me with his mild blue eyes, holding the teapot in his two hands, about to set it on the table. *I—I didn't know we could hear you!* I blurted out, delighted, and he smiled a beautiful smile and nodded his head. Then he began to sing again, and I awoke with the tune in my head. Such a happy thing, it was; I lay there with the music for what seemed like a long time, until at last it faded away. *I didn't know we could hear you.*

Just a dream, of course. They seem so real, but they prove nothing to someone who does not already believe. How do we know there is anything at all beyond this life? Can we prove it? No, we can't. We who believe don't have some secret knowledge, some information hidden to others.

But we do have the power to decide, and the power to base our decisions on the decades of the life we're living now, the past and future of it. We do have our longings, on which we base our faith decisions, at least in part. We have dreams, like mine of my dad, moments of touching something else, if only for an instant. We have the record of other people's moments recorded in scripture, people who thought them important enough to write down. We have new scientific and mathematical knowledge of the smallness of our existence, and of an unanticipated order in seemingly chaotic events. All these things puzzle us, darting around in our experience like fireflies on a summer night. We cannot help but see them. And we cannot help but use them.

MONDAY IN LENT III

Pss 80 * 77, (79)
Genesis 44:18–34
1 Corinthians 7:25–31
Mark 5:21–43

*Immediately aware that power had gone forth from him,
Jesus turned about in the crowd and said,
"Who touched my clothes?"*
MARK 5:30

What a story—an important person's urgent request is postponed in its fulfillment by a poor sick old woman who doesn't even have a reservation, with disastrous results: The synagogue leader's little girl *dies* waiting for Jesus to come.

But Jesus was busy: A healing has happened. He felt it coming from him. The poor woman who touched the hem of his garment was terrified when he asked to know who had received the healing; she confessed "in fear and trembling," we are told. Not only has she touched an important person and transmitted the ritual uncleanness that is hers because she is hemorrhaging to him, she has interfered with the needs of an important person. Surely this is it. She will be punished.

But no. Nobody is punished. Not the poor woman and not the rich man's little girl, either. There is enough healing to go around. Rich and poor, pure and ritually soiled, old and young, important and anonymous: Jesus is no respecter of rank. His power is for everyone.

And notice that his power costs him something—it is free for the asking to everyone else, but he feels it leave him. He spends it, and then it is replenished, over and over again. Probably he got tired from his healings—we see him resting, now and then. He is not Superman. He is a real man.

And he is really God. How is this so? Scripture never tells us how—the people who wrote it didn't know, either. But the stories of healings point to a moment when sickness and death are gone, when the differences between rich and poor are gone. When there are no important people and no unimportant ones. Just all of us, all together. All in all and all in Christ, all the people of the world.

TUESDAY IN LENT III

Pss 78:1–19 * 78:40–72
Genesis 45:1–15
1 Corinthians 7:32–40
Mark 6:1–13

*And he wept so loudly that the Egyptians heard it,
and the household of Pharoah heard it.*
GENESIS 45:2

Oops. Sometimes a hotel's walls are just a mite too thin, and you hear an encounter you really weren't meant to hear. Sometimes you mistakenly receive an e-mail intended for someone else and read something in it you're really not supposed to know. Sometimes a colleague in the cubicle next to yours forgets that you can hear her talking to her spouse, and you hear something that really wasn't for your ears. In the old days there were party lines on the telephone—ask your parents if you don't remember this—and we kids used to love to eavesdrop on people's conversations.

Joseph wanted some privacy when he revealed himself to his brothers; it was a family moment. But even though everyone else in the household left them alone together, he made so much noise weeping that the whole house must have wondered what was up. I suppose nobody said much when he emerged from the room, his eyes red and puffy. He was still Joseph, and he was still in charge. But this was a side of Joseph the people who worked for him had never seen.

I was in the hospital, and had been for days. I couldn't walk, and so couldn't have a shower. At last I could have a sponge bath, and I was lying there with a little tub of water and a cake of soap and a washcloth on the table next to me, wondering how I was going to manage, when a colleague came in for a visit. We liked each other, but we weren't best friends of years' standing, and we weren't sisters.

I couldn't help it: *Could you help me take a bath?* I blurted out, and of course she helped me: soaped the washcloth and then rinsed it, over and over, until I was finished. *It feels so good to be clean again,* I said, *thanks so much. Sure,* she said.

It had not been our relationship, such physical intimacy. Such vulnerability and weakness on my part. Certainly, it was a side of me she had never seen. But it didn't matter. I was still me and she was still herself. To this day, I am grateful.

WEDNESDAY IN LENT III

Pss 119:97–120 * 81, 82
Genesis 45:16–28
1 Corinthians 8:1–13
Mark 6:13–29

"John, whom I beheaded, has been raised."
MARK 6:16

Herod is like Lady Macbeth—he fears that his sin will follow him, and so he sees it everywhere, even in places where it is not. His guilty conscience doesn't keep him from digging himself in even deeper, though: Soon he will compound his sin in the role he plays in Jesus' execution.

Usually, guilt doesn't keep us from sin. It makes us secretive: We don't want anyone to know what we've done. But it doesn't make us *change*. Our secretiveness serves only to protect and preserve our sin, to preserve the way to it. Something else is required for change to happen.

We need repentance if we are to change. Not just the conviction that we have done wrong, but the conviction that we can do something else. That we can live another way, and that we *want* to live another way. This isn't going to be possible under our own power alone—it was while relying on our *own* power that we got ourselves into our mess. Repentance will be despair until we think that there is a power beyond ourselves that can help us do what we cannot seem to manage on our own.

And there is. Talk to someone who is open about his healing from addiction. Talk with someone who has survived a scandal and can be honest about it. Talk with someone who sabotaged her own marriage and got another chance. We don't always do very well on our own. But we are not on our own. Those who have come back from graves of their own digging know that they didn't make it back alone.

THURSDAY IN LENT III

Pss (83) or 42, 43 * 85, 86
Genesis 46:1–7, 28–34
1 Corinthians 9:1–15
Mark 6:30–46

Indeed, I would rather die than that—no one will
deprive me of my ground for boasting!
1 CORINTHIANS 9:15

Right. Well, at least Paul is honest: He has spent the whole chapter complaining about how hard his life is and how little respect he gets, and then winds it up by insisting that he doesn't want to change any of that, that he wants to go on being poor and lonely and ignored.

You may be familiar with this rhetoric. You may have even employed it—*Oh, just never mind*, you may have said, *Don't worry about me. Just go on about your business like you always do anyhow.*

Here's the truth: God is not glorified by our being mistreated or by our mistreating ourselves. Being bitter and deprived praises God not at all. If you can't deprive yourself without being bitter and martyred, maybe you shouldn't deprive yourself at all. If your Lenten fast makes you mean to everyone around you, then eat something, for God's sake.

Have you ever received a gift from someone who hated giving gifts? Could you feel the deprivation she felt in having to hand it over? Wasn't it hard to experience any delight in the gift at all—didn't it feel like the price tag was still attached, weren't you so aware of her sacrifice that you really wished she hadn't bothered? Didn't it feel like a business deal?

The delight of the recipient is the sole reason for any gift. That delight delights the giver, and it is delight enough.

FRIDAY IN LENT III

Pss 95, 88 * 91, 92
Genesis 47:1–26
1 Corinthians 9:16–27
Mark 6:47–56

And they were utterly astounded,
for they did not understand about the loaves,
but their hearts were hardened.
MARK 6:51–52

Huh? They were astonished to see Jesus walking on the water because they didn't understand *about the loaves*? What do the loaves have to do with this?

Well, we *did* just finish reading about the feeding of the five thousand in the verses immediately preceding these verses, and there *were* actual loaves of bread in that story.

There was a general feeling of helplessness, there among all those people: We have nothing to give them, we are miles from anywhere, and they are hungry. We have come to the end of our ability. And it was the same situation on the lake: The rowing is hard and we are making little headway. We are doing our very best and it just isn't good enough.

And we see two miraculous solutions to these insoluble problems, things we don't ordinarily see. In the hyperbolic language of Jesus' miracles, these amazements point toward the reversal of earth's limitations and sorrows. Something more than human power is at work in the world, they tell us. Don't think you're on your own here. Learn to depend on God in every moment of life— you will be rewarded, not with a miracle a minute, but with a life lived in complete trust, a life free of anxiety and despair.

The meaning of a miracle isn't that I'm going to get out of every bad situation in which I find myself. However many amazing near-miss brushes with death I may have in my life, I'm going to end up dying someday and I won't be able to get out of it. All the men in the boat that day died eventually, on some other day, and so did every last one of the five thousand people who ate the miraculous bread.

So live. Live in fear of failure, sickness, want and death, or live trusting in God. We get to choose which it will be.

SATURDAY IN LENT III

Pss 87, 90 * 136
Genesis 47:27–48:7
1 Corinthians 10:1–13
Mark 7:1–23

I do not want you to be unaware. . . .
1 CORINTHIANS 10:1

Many of the people relaxing on the beach must have had cell phones—most of them were people of some means. But, of course, they were on vacation—maybe they didn't have their phones with them. But somebody in the hotel was near a phone: Why didn't somebody call with a warning about the tsunami?

Maybe they did. But the water was blue and calm, and the sky was blue, without a cloud, and the sun was shining. This was paradise, so far from the dark of the Swedish winter, so far from New York and Pennsylvania and Frankfurt. This was the life.

Turn and look out at the calm sea: An enormous wave is steaming toward you right now. It will be here in minutes. Run for your life.

Nah. Everything is fine. Just look at that sea—not a ripple.

Obesity kills people. *I am forty pounds overweight. But I feel fine.* Sometimes heart attacks are signaled by just the slightest tightening in the chest, not by sudden severe pain. *I have a little tightening in my chest. But I know it's not a heart attack. How do I know? I just know, that's all. I'm fine.* Cigarettes kill people. *I still smoke. But I feel okay.* Extramarital affairs usually end marriages. *This one won't, though. I can handle things.*

We get plenty of warnings. But they warn us of things we cannot see, not yet, and so we don't really believe in them. Mostly we have a means of escape from disaster, but we don't try to use it before it comes. We try to get away when it's already here, and by then it's too late. Who knows—maybe other people got the same warning about the rains to come that Noah got. Maybe the signs were everywhere. Maybe nobody but Noah believed them.

To believe before the evidence forces us to believe, to act before there is any evidence, to listen to a warning and act on it solely because of trust in the one who brings it: That's rare in human affairs. But almost every instance of God breaking into our history is like that: Mary learns of her pregnancy before it happens, John sees Jesus as the Messiah before he looks like anything but a man very like John himself. We cannot imagine our own end, and we don't wish to hear about it.

But there are warnings. Listen up.

SUNDAY, LENT IV

Pss 66, 67 * 19, 46
Genesis 48:8–22
Romans 8:11–25
John 6:27–40

*"Very truly, I tell you, it was not Moses who gave
you the bread from heaven, but is my Father
who gives you the true bread from heaven."*
JOHN 6:32

Moses would have agreed. The miraculous bread of the Exodus came from God, along with everything else. Moses was not a person who sought his own glory.

Neither was Jesus. That was an aspect of his personality that puzzled everyone around him: He seemed uninterested in reaping the benefits of his fame.

It's interesting, then, that his followers couldn't seem to let that part of him be. He couldn't seem to wean them from the notions of power and grandeur they entertained about him. Perhaps they sensed a deficit of earthly power in themselves—and they would have been right about that, certainly, since not a man among them counted for much of anything in terms of wealth or power—and wanted him to compensate for it. Simple working people themselves, they nevertheless wanted *him* to become a king.

I know people who are uncomfortable giving praise to God. It seems to them to detract from human dignity. *God is good!* I might say when Tom does something wonderful. *So is Tom!* will come back the response, almost as a rebuke, as if I had forgotten to give credit where credit is due. But it is glorious for Tom and everyone else to understand that we are part of God's glory every time we act in a Christlike manner. Every good thing we do, from the small kindnesses to the really big sacrifices, is a glorious part of what God does. That doesn't *detract* from our dignity; it locates it squarely where it actually lives.

The closer our walk with God, the more dignity we will have. And the less anxious we will be about our own place on the marquee.

MONDAY IN LENT IV

Pss 89:1–18 * 89:19–52
Genesis 49:1–28
1 Corinthians 10:14–11:1
Mark 7:24–37

*"He has done everything well; he even makes the
deaf to hear and the mute to speak."*
MARK 7:37

And here we see the limits of miracles: People will focus on them instead of on the one who interrupts the laws of nature to permit them, and grow no closer to God as a result of them. That's why Jesus is shy about his own miracles and implores people not to publicize them; he rightly fears a feeding frenzy.

When we see evidence that God is active in human history, we immediately hope that we can harness that power in our own behalf. *God is mighty; perhaps I can find a way to make sure God is mighty for me.* This person was healed of disease, that one got her sight back—shouldn't I rightly expect a speedy end to my own troubles?

The logic of this line of thought turns God into a powerful but obedient genie, who has only to hear of our troubles before he makes them disappear. Focus on the miracles of Jesus alone and you lose the life of Jesus—a life that did not end in a nimble leap from the cross, but in real death and real defeat.

Jesus isn't just someone who does a lot of things really well. To defeat death he must enter it, as we will. He enters weakness and pain, too, all the weaknesses and pains we can have, he enters. Sometimes they end and one day they won't, and we will die of them. Every single one of the people he healed miraculously went on to die in some other way—not a one of them is still alive. The miracles get our attention, but we must go deeper if we are to find out what they really mean.

TUESDAY IN LENT IV

Pss 97, 99, (100) * 94, (95)
Genesis 49:29–50:14
1 Corinthians 11:17–34
Mark 8:1–10

*After he had buried his father, Joseph returned
to Egypt with his brothers and all who had
gone up with him to bury his father.*
GENESIS 50:14

Our forebears in faith were economic refugees. There was a famine at home, so Jacob and all his children moved to Egypt, where they would work as shepherds, work no Egyptian wanted to do.

I see them every morning, handsome young Mexican men getting off the train and walking to their jobs as gardeners. It is a trade they have all but taken over here. They are essential: people who will do work Americans will not do. Essential, and yet they are viewed with suspicion: They steal, Anglos tell each other, they're lazy, stupid, they can't be trusted. Every ethnic group arriving on our shores has been described this way—Germans, Irish, Italian—while, at the same time, Americans have eagerly bought their services for far less than they themselves would have been willing to accept.

Stupid, shiftless, lazy, crooked: It is as if we felt the need to invent moral reasons for treating these newcomers poorly, think of some rationale by which they deserve it. These days, we equate immigration with terrorism, and there are calls to close our borders altogether.

That's just how the Egyptians felt about the Hebrews: They hated them and they needed them, a sub-class upon whose backs they could maintain their prosperous lifestyle. We think we're the children of Israel in this story. Wouldn't it be something if we turned out to be the children of Pharoah, instead?

WEDNESDAY IN LENT IV

Pss 101, 109:1–4 (5–19) 20–30 * 119:121–144
Genesis 50:15–26
1 Corinthians 12:1–11
Mark 8:11–26

*You know that when you were pagans, you were enticed
and led astray to idols that could not speak.*
1 CORINTHIANS 12:2

The church was proud of its edginess: *We are a church where people who hate church can feel welcome*, the people said. It was proud of its avant-garde character. But sometimes it seemed to me to enjoy the effect it had on newcomers a little more than was healthy. I didn't think, for instance, that the photograph of two shirtless women on a motorcycle was necessarily the best thing to attract families with children, which was one of the things the people said they wanted to do.

So it was tense, sometimes, proffering a simultaneous welcome to artistic, left-leaning urbanites and to the conservative Hispanic families whose children attended the after-school program.

We really are free in Christ. You really can't sin your way out of the embrace of his love. And faith really is more than conformity to middle-class good manners. There really is nothing sinful about two topless women on a motorcycle.

And yet. And yet—it wasn't just church-shy baby boomers to whom we ministered.

It was parents trying to raise children who would respect their bodies as the temple of God. The difference between enshrining a leering gaze and celebrating the beauty of the human body, clearly accessible to a forty-five-year-old actor or community organizer, would be lost on a five-year-old. We grow into these things.

Censorship! A few cried when I raised the issue. *Cowardice!*

Maybe. I was hoping, though, to navigate the treacherous shoals of art and nurture, courage and caution. It isn't always true that we should do everything we can do. We're not in the business of faith for ourselves alone, after all. We're in it for each other.

THURSDAY IN LENT IV

Pss 69:1–23 (24–30) 31–38 * 73
Exodus 1:6–22
1 Corinthians 23:12-26
Mark 8:27-9:1

Now a new king arose over Egypt,
who did not know Joseph.
EXODUS 1:8

That's it, right there: a one-sentence explanation for how we get from the miraculous resettlement of Joseph and his brothers in Goshen to their descendents living in an apartheid-like arrangement as slaves to the Egyptians, and the stage is set for the great drama of deliverance that defines the Jewish people's relationship to God.

How did the British come to dominate India? Through their powerful trading companies of the eighteenth century, which solidified safe passage for trade and cheap manufacture through bargains with local rulers. They ended up owning everything, even though they were utterly outnumbered.

Africans and Vietnamese speaking French. Filipinos learning Spanish, and then blending it into Tagalog. Brazilians with Japanese surnames who speak Portuguese. Bosnians who speak a little bit of everything, because you just never know. It's amazing where a group of people can end up in this world. And how much power they can lose, and how quickly. And how integral to their national soul is their longing for home and language and kindred.

Whenever I send out a meditation that touches, however tangentially, on politics, I can count on a handful of stiff messages back asking me not to talk about politics, please. But there isn't a spiritual situation in which a human being finds herself that doesn't have something to do with political arrangements. We live in the world, and there are other people in it in—therefore, by definition, *politics*. If you want a faith that you can exercise without thinking about politics, I'm not sure where you should go. I can't think of one.

I think I get the mail because people sense that I hold a position that disagrees with one they hold, and it troubles them. *How can I like her if we don't agree about politics? How can I hold a spiritual conversation with her if we don't see eye to eye about the temporal world?* Well, *easily*: I like many people with whom I disagree. Learn more from them, often, than I do from those whose sentence I could finish.

Don't surround yourself with yes-men and yes-women. Don't spend all your time in your own amen corner. There's not much there you don't already know.

FRIDAY IN LENT IV

Pss 95, 102 * 107:1–32
Exodus 2:1–22
1 Corinthians 12:27–13:3
Mark 9:2–13

And he was transfigured before them. . . .
MARK 9:2

Are you scared about it? my friend asks over our coffee. We have just finished lunch on a trip down memory lane to a place near our seminary. Besides the coffee, we are also sharing a Brownie All the Way. As you can no doubt imagine, nothing in a Brownie All the Way is in my eating plan, but I haven't had one since 1979, so it's probably okay.

Well, sort of. But I really feel fine, so I'm just taking it day by day. We are talking about my latest neurological diagnosis, which is a long time coming. I have hydrocephalus—water on the brain—for no apparent reason and with, as yet, no protocol for treatment. Its end result, if treatment is impossible, is dementia. Its only treatment is a shunt, draining the excess fluid safely away from the brain to the abdomen. Not all hydrocephalus can be treated with a shunt. We're trying to find out if mine can. I hope so.

But actually, I am more interested than afraid. In illness, one learns a great deal about the body and its mysteries and a great deal about oneself. About fear and what happens after fear.

What I have learned from fear is this: you can walk through it and come out on the other side. You can see beyond the worst thing that can happen into a reality beyond that worst thing: this is not all there is, this world with its joys and sorrows. To have been here at all is a tremendous blessing for each of us. Disability and change don't undo the blessing, although people who don't have disabilities always think it surely must.

I'm going to have repeated tests in which they ask you who the president is and make you count backwards by sevens.

Can you count backwards by sevens?

Sort of. I can't remember where I was last weekend, though.

Well, who can? True enough. Everyone middle-aged person I know is worried about short-term memory loss. *Maybe we all have hydrocephalus.*

Yeah, maybe we do. It is time to get back to work. He pays the bill and we leave the place.

Life itself is a process of Transfiguration—we are being changed, all our lives long. The final change takes us out of this existence and into the larger one, but all our changes change us. None of us is what she was. Or what she will be. You might as well get up and see what's going on, while you still can. And nothing is to be gained by being afraid, and much is lost: all delight in what remains, enjoyed only by those who will pay attention to it and drink deeply from the bittersweet chalice of life.

SATURDAY IN LENT IV

Pss 107:33–43, 108:1–6 (7–13) * 33
Exodus 2:23–3:15
1 Corinthians 13:1–13
Mark 9:14–29

"This kind can come out only through prayer."
MARK 9:29

Well, *I guess there's nothing to do now but pray,* someone will say when someone else is gravely ill. The implication is that prayer itself is next to nothing. And it feels like that, to us, since prayer isn't all about our expertise and our energy. We don't *do* prayer. We're not in control in prayer. This we don't like. No wonder prayer feels like nothing to us: We didn't invent it.

But the truth is that there really has always been nothing to do but pray. All of our muscular interventions in the machinery of life have always been conducted within the framework of God's gift— we don't have a thing that God didn't give us. This was already true, has always been true, since before your dear one was injured, before she became ill.

And so does this mean that if we remain in a constant state of prayer nothing bad will ever happen to us? Well, we know better than *that.* But I will be able to accept what comes to me, without outrage or panic, if my life is lived in the steady awareness that I am in God's care at every moment. And I will *have* that steady aware-ness if I get in the habit of taking myself there by the process of remembering, wondering, and truth-telling that is prayer.

But what is the *means* by which this happens? I have thought about it a great deal, and have come to the conclusion that the grat-itude that builds steadily when we pray steadily puts sorrow into perspective. Life is indeed hard, but it is also beautiful and we are blessed to be here at all—hardly any of us want to leave! And so we lose the sense of entitlement, so easily tipped toward grievance, that accompanied us before we really thought things through. We had none of this coming, it turns out. It turns out that we were entitled to none of it. Everything is gift, and nothing is to be expected. Events come and go throughout life, and we receive them all, for good and for ill, within a loving embrace.

SUNDAY, LENT V

Pss 118 * 145
Exodus 3:16–4:12
Romans 12:1–21
John 8:46–59

Beloved, never avenge yourselves, but leave room
for the wrath of God; for it is written, "Vengeance
is mine, I will repay, says the Lord."
ROMANS 12:19

*R*oom for the wrath of God. It is supposed to replace our own wrath, to be a court of higher jurisdiction to which all our crusades can be referred. It sounds as if God were like us: bad-tempered, tending toward anger and retribution. As if God were wrathful, as wrathful as we are when we have been injured.

But the wrath of God can only live within the context of the righteousness of God. An arms race of retribution, an eye for an eye for an eye for an eye for an eye, with no end in sight—these things are too human to be part of the divine vengeance. They tend toward greater and greater death, and God is the author of greater and greater life.

The wrath of God scours the earth, for sometimes that is what must happen before something new and good can take root. The wrath of God is educational; it prepares us for the changes God has in mind for us, changes our behavior has made necessary. The wrath of God isn't something God chooses initially—it is we who make it necessary, all on our own, by the acts of injustice we heap upon each other.

Things like volcanoes, tsunamis, earthquakes—these things are not the wrath of God: They are natural occurrences of weather and topography. The just and the unjust alike lose lives and property in these events. But some of them are re-formed in the midst of the suffering of these things, and we glimpse God's mysterious, mighty hand at work.

MONDAY IN LENT V

Pss 31 * 35
Exodus 4:10–20 (21–26) 27–31
1 Corinthians 14:1–19
Mark 9:30–41

Then he took a little child and put it among them; and taking
it in his arms, he said to them, "Whoever welcomes
one such child in my name welcomes me . . ."
MARK 9:36–37

This child—he or she sounds a great deal more *portable* in the gospel of Mark than the child we remember from the pictures we have seen of this moment: usually it is a five-year-old we see in those Bible pictures. But this child stays put, right where Jesus puts him as if he were a sack of flour, and then Jesus picks him up and cuddles him. It sounds to me like the child is a *baby*.

Which would make this rather a different story, wouldn't it? A baby is a bundle of helplessness, a small package of mystery whose future is completely unknown. A baby has done nothing, yet, to complicate his original innocence. A baby can't live without love and nurture. Welcome a baby and you're accepting life itself, fragile life, and the unstinting commitment life requires.

And a baby necessarily lives in community—if the baby has no community in which to live, she dies. Welcome a baby and you welcome the baby's family—they come with him. You don't love a baby in a vacuum: You must love the family of which the baby is the newest hope, the mother who bore the baby, the father who cares for his family—everyone, in whatever configuration of familial love the baby arrives, who is charged with seeing to it that she reaches adulthood in one piece.

Jesus picks up the baby, gives her a gentle cuddle and hands her back to her mother, who also cuddles her close. Welcome the baby and the baby's family, and soon you will be welcoming the world.

TUESDAY IN LENT V

Pss (120), 121, 122, 123 * 124, 125, 126, (127)
Exodus 5:1–6:1
1 Corinthians 14:20–33a, 39–40
Mark 9:42–50

. . . do not be children in your thinking; rather,
be infants in evil, but in thinking be adults.
1 CORINTHIANS 14:20

Childlike, but not childish. An interesting distinction. People return to church after a long absence—or come to it as adults for the first time—hardly daring to believe in the hope that reawakens within them: Here I have found unconditional love, here my gifts are honored. Here my wounds will be healed, at long last. They meet Jesus, perhaps for the first time, and he accepts them completely for who they are.

Good and powerful stuff, acceptance and welcome: These things are in short supply in the world of adults. Suddenly you're home again, after years away. *I love this church,* someone will say, misting up a little; *it's like my family.*

It is only a step or two from feeling like a child at home to acting like one. *This is my church. It needs to stay the way I like it. This is my seat. Find your own.*

But church isn't a second chance to right old wrongs from the days when we were at home in our families of origin. We grow out of our conviction that the world is centered on us, and church isn't a second chance at re-creating that ancient paradise. We're children of God, all right, but we're not children.

It's not a surprise that people tend to regress in churches: God is our father, our mother, the endlessly patient and loving father and mother no human father or mother ever is. Such trustworthiness fills us with a renewed sense of how dependent we are on God, as dependent as babies. But that dependence is spiritual. It doesn't mean we get to be kids again in the flesh. Or in our minds. Or in our organizations. That childhood really *is* over.

WEDNESDAY IN LENT V

Pss 119:145–176 * 128, 129, 130
Exodus 7:8–24
2 Corinthians 2:14–3:6
Mark 10:1–16

For we are the aroma of Christ . . .
2 CORINTHIANS 2:15

The celebrant spoons incense into the pot and immediately it begins to smoke, the fragrant layers of it suspended in the air, rising slowly toward the high ceiling. The smell is deep and holy—it is intended to remind us of our prayers ascending to heaven, and to link us with the worshipers of our ancient past.

But a muffled chant begins in corners of the church: conspicuous, aggrieved coughing and throat clearing. Most of this is political, not medical: Some people just don't like incense in church and don't want anyone else to have it, either. Ah, well. You can't please everybody, and there are some people you can't please no matter what. The priest will just have to figure it out.

Incense is a powerful part of my prayer at home. I can pray without it, but its lovely layers rising from the embers, the ancient smell of the Middle East it brings into my little office—these things widen the tiny room, bring other ages and other places into it. And incense reminds me of a world I do not know, one nobody knows, the one into whose mysterious heights the smoke rises and disappears from view, leaving only the faint aroma of prayers offered centuries ago, and just this morning, lingering in the air.

What senses remain in the next world? None of them, I suppose: They are physical, and we are spiritual there and don't need them. No, they are for us here, now, little bits of delight to bring us joy, lift us higher, stir our memories, tell us things we can't know any other way. Every scrap of sensual beauty in the world is an earnest of the spiritual beauty to come. Even now, we breathe God in with each breath; incense reminds us that this is so.

THURSDAY IN LENT V

Pss 131, 132, (133) * 140, 142
Exodus 7:25–8:19
2 Corinthians 3:7–18
Mark 10:17–31

When he heard this, he was shocked and went away grieving, for he had many possessions.
MARK 10:22

How much am I willing to lose? Just the extras? What if it were everything? No wonder the rich young man was sad.

It is said that the great Russian writer Leo Tolstoy did that: gave away everything he had at the end of his life. The French philosopher and mathematician Blaise Pascal did it, too. They wanted to enter fully into the life of Christ and understood being unencumbered by their wealth as an important first step.

Both men were very wealthy, as most of us are not. I wonder if it was not the gulf between the young man's situation and the poverty of many of his neighbors, rather than the fact of having possessions at all, that stood in the way of his progress in holiness. Could he become willing to deprive himself for the sake of a stranger? If he could not, it would be hard for him to follow Christ.

No, we are not rich in comparison to the rich young man or Leo Tolstoy. But we're fabulously wealthy in comparison with almost everybody else in the world. It is difficult for Americans to brook even the smallest diminution in lifestyle or comfort—we *must* have our enormous cars, our air conditioners, our dozens of pairs of shoes. Could we reduce our riches in order to lift the lot of the poor?

Our record isn't good here. We'll give of what we have to spare. But we won't deprive ourselves. Not in the least.

FRIDAY IN LENT V

Pss 95, 22 * 141, 143:1–11 (12)
Exodus 9:13–35
2 Corinthians 4:1–12
Mark 10:32–45

Therefore, since it is by God's mercy that we are engaged
in this ministry, we do not lose heart.
2 CORINTHIANS 4:1

Things don't always go well in ministry. Probably 50 percent of what you try fails to bear noticeable fruit. Your idealism wars with your strength, urging you onward to greater and greater perfection and shaking its head in disapproval at all the shortcomings in your vocation. You depend on others, and sometimes they don't come through. And sometimes you yourself are all wrong about something, and its failure is exactly what should happen.

But don't lose heart. Everyone has reversals. The best among us has moments of failure. Whether it arises from your own shortfall or someone else's, you will often have to pick up the tab for it.

I hate to fail. More than anything, I hate to fail. I am a harsh self-critic, and my failures are huge in my own eyes. But they do nothing at all to disturb God's love for me, or God's gentle guidance of me and the people I touch, even if I get things wrong and make things temporarily worse by my mighty efforts. Up to and including our own death, there are no messes we can get into from which God cannot bring us into growth and goodness.

Thanks. Thanks for rescuing me. Thanks for showing me what I did wrong and what I did right. Thanks for setting me on another path. Thanks for helping me with my humility deficit. Thanks for comforting me when things are my fault and when they're not. Thanks for helping me not to lose heart.

SATURDAY IN LENT V

Pss 137:1–6 (7–9), 144 * 42, 43
Exodus 10:21–11:8
2 Corinthians 4:13–18
Mark 10:46–52

*Even though our outer nature is wasting away,
our inner nature is being renewed day by day.*
2 CORINTHIANS 4:16

7:15? I *never* sleep until 7:15. *Well, we must have been tired*, Q says comfortably, stretching carefully so as not to topple Noodle from her perch on his chest, where she is watching his face intently. She is attempting to transmit thought telepathically: Noodle wants her breakfast in the morning, and wonders what's taking us so *long* today.

Slower in the morning—I can no longer count on long, quiet hours of prayer and writing between 4 a.m. and when everyone else arises. Is this sloth or true weariness?

Should I be struggling to subdue it or assume my body is telling me something worth hearing and give in?

7:15 and I haven't sent out a "Howdy do?" let alone a "Let us bless the Lord," I tell Q.

They'll be all right, he says. *Send it when you get there.* And soon it *is* out, and the answering "Thanks be to God" begin to appear.

They are like the roosters I used to hear in the mornings when I was young; another day on the Farm begins.

Can't do what you used to do the way you used to do it? Maybe you can do it another way. Noodle looks uncomfortable when I talk about there being more than one way to skin a cat besides putting hot butter down its ears, but it is true: There are many paths to the things we really want to do and be. God specializes in many paths: Over and over in scripture, human beings ruin things and God provides another way. God never runs out of ways in which to allow us to grow into his image. God's imagination is bigger than ours, but ours are better than most of us think they are, once we get them in gear.

Don't give up: Pay attention. There's something you haven't thought of yet, some alternative way—or maybe an alternative goal—that will bless you every bit as much as the one you thought was the only one you could have.

Holy Week

PALM SUNDAY

Pss 24, 29 * 103
Zechariah 9:9–12 * Zechariah 12:9–11, 13:1, 7–9
1 Timothy 6:12–16
Luke 19:41–48

. . . Christ Jesus, who in his testimony before
Pontius Pilate made the good confession . . .
1 TIMOTHY 6:13

As you recall, Jesus barely spoke to Pilate—a few words, some remarks about power and where it comes from. Not a word in his own defense. Paul wasn't there that day, as far as we know. The accounts of the Passion are the oldest parts of the gospels as we have them—if Jesus had been more talkative at that crucial moment, it seems that one of them would have recorded his words. We can assume he just didn't say much.

Besides, there really wasn't much to say: He had a task ahead of him, not a speaking engagement. Mightn't we expect that he would be like we would be at such a moment: terrified? Afraid to speak, for fear he might begin to weep? Courage does not cancel out fear; it just moves forward in spite of it. He must have felt plenty of fear.

The "good confession" before Pilate was not really a confession in words. It was his self-giving submission to unjust power in order to transform its categories forever. Now we will see what it means for the last to be first. We are about to find out how it is that the meek inherit the earth.

Young Timothy faced the same fearful future. So did Paul, who wrote to him. So did they all, thousands of them: They could see it coming. Christ had become *who they were,* and they knew they could no longer live if living meant living without him. Great power may have killed them, but they chose to face it in order to remain truly themselves.

Are you likely to be martyred for your faith? Probably not, but you are certain to die, and are called to decide just who it is who will be making the crossing.

MONDAY IN HOLY WEEK

Pss 51:1–18 (19–20) * 69:1–23
Lamentations 1:1–2, 6–12
2 Corinthians 1:1–17
Mark 11:12–25

Is it nothing to you, all you who pass by?
LAMENTATIONS 1:12

One of the hardest things about a catastrophic sorrow is its ongoing loneliness. A sincere but brief flurry of love and support, and then you're on your own. People who don't know you can't tell what happened by looking at you; even those who do know can't see into your heart. Besides, they have their own hearts to attend to. And so they pass by. It's not really *nothing* to them: It's just that, in the end, it's not *their* sorrow. It's yours.

Bereft of human companionship in grief, it is difficult to learn to find comfort in the divine love. That one special person is what you want: We're not built to *feel* God the way we feel other human beings. Quickly, you realize that "feeling" God will be something new, a love other than all your other loves. For one thing, it *elasticizes* us, stretching, encompassing everything we are and everything we feel, joy and sorrow alike. It *contains* everything.

And for another, it's permanent. Forever, and after forever. It's not going to be ripped from us, leaving us to bleed and weep.

It takes a while to begin to see and feel this elastic love. It takes some patience—you live through some very dark and lonely eras before you begin to notice the light of it, begin to feel its warmth. It is not like other loves, and you realize that all your other loves taught you something of it. That you have always been on your way to it.

TUESDAY IN HOLY WEEK

Pss 6, 12 * 94
Lamentations 1:17–22
2 Corinthians 1:8–22
Mark 11:27–33

For in him every one of God's promises is a "Yes."
2 CORINTHIANS 1:20

Late winter snow is heavier than midwinter snow: It has more water. It clumps on the plants and the tree branches like scoops of ice cream.

And it is heavier to shovel, a fact that inspires my seven-thousandth attempt to persuade Q to hire someone to do the driveway and the sidewalk out front. Neither of us feels well this morning—he hurt his leg last week and has a chest cold, and I have a chest cold, too. I point out these things to him, but—perhaps because I'm just too tired—I don't put as much energy into the argument as I usually do. I don't, for instance, bring up the many men who die shoveling snow. I don't say anything scornful about WASP machismo. The talk is gentler than any of the fights we've had about snow shoveling in all these years. It is not settled when we finish talking.

But when he comes in from clearing the front and back steps and feeding the birds, he tells me that he hailed the neighbor boy and his snowblower and engaged him for the public walk and the driveway. Five bucks, five minutes and it's clear.

All those arguments. All my worry and anger. Finished in five dollars and five minutes.

Yesterday, Prime Minister Sharon announced the closing of several settlements in Gaza. After all the arguments about them, all these years, all that pain, all that anger, all the killings. There will be a political cost to him at home—a big one—but peace can never come there without this step. And the Israelis also announced that they will stop bulldozing the homes of suicide bombers' families, a practice that is at least twenty years old. They said what so many have said: It didn't seem to be helping end the bombings. Just like that. After all these years.

So things can change. People can come together and do something other than what they've always done. We can change our minds.

When does Christ come? When do things turn around? When is enough finally enough? What makes you decide to do something else, now, after all these years? It's different for each person, certainly—that's why we argue about things: We don't see things the same way. But we can *come* to see them, and we can change our minds and do something else.

WEDNESDAY IN HOLY WEEK

Pss 55 * 74
Lamentations 2:1–9
2 Corinthians 1:23–2:11
Mark 12:1–11

*"The stone that the builders rejected
has become the cornerstone. . . ."*
MARK 12:10

My part was a small one—one scene. A handful of lines and actions—I was a nurse, engaged to care for the Elephant Man, who couldn't handle either his appearance or his stench. That was about the extent of my role.

You know, said Lee Winston, after watching me do a mediocre job in my small part, *in a role like that—one in which you do one scene and the audience never sees you again—you're the star of that one scene. Its only reason is for you to be there and tell the audience what it is you know—the playwright wouldn't have put your character in the play if that character didn't have something to say the audience needs to hear and that only she can say. So take the stage. It's may be only one scene, but it's not a small part.*

I never forgot what he told me. He was absolutely right, I saw immediately: Only we can do what we do, and we are each the star of the scene we're in. Maybe we're not the star of the whole play—but our scene is our scene.

It's important to be important, I guess. But not everyone is called to high visibility—in fact, hardly any of us are. Almost all of us work our way through life and faith considerably below the radar of public awareness. Not many people know about us. But God knows about all of it.

MAUNDY THURSDAY

Pss 102 * 142, 143
Lamentations 2:10–18
1 Corinthians 10:14–17; 11:27–32
Mark 14:12–25

*Because there is one bread, we who are many are
one body, for we all partake of the one bread.*
1 CORINTHIANS 10:17

Never have I heard of such a thing: putting loaves of bread into a cold oven and then turning it on to bake. I guess they get an extra rise on their way up to 400 degrees. Well, I just put them in, so we shall soon see.

There are so many ways to make bread: with rotting sourdough starter, with dry yeast, with cake yeast, with no yeast at all. So many ways to shape it: in braids, in wheels, in long baguettes, in plain round loaves. So many flour combinations, so many different liquids and fats. So many things you can put in it: raisins, nuts, dates, prunes, chocolate. The staff of life is infinitely variable.

This is my body, Jesus says, as he breaks the loaf for the evening meal. He does it in Jerusalem in the first century and he does it at the church across the street from our house and in Africa and in

Papua, New Guinea in the twenty-first. Round white wafers that resemble fish food and stick to the roof of your mouth if you're not careful. Sweet brown loaves made by the Sunday school kids. A New York bagel, a Middle Eastern round of pita. Any bread can be the bread of the Eucharist, any humble food sanctified to this holy use.

We all have different ideas of Jesus, too, along with all our different breads. We all read the same gospels, but each of us sees a different Christ, the one he needs to see. Christ can come to us like that—as various as we are.

So we'd better be careful with him, gentle in our approach to another person's Jesus. We haven't walked in that person's shoes. We aren't qualified to prescribe the manner in which he is allowed to experience Christ. That is between each of us and God. Our only task is to experience all our different Christs together, to worship him together, to talk about him together, so that we can grow from our love for Christ and for each other, regardless of our differences.

GOOD FRIDAY

Pss 95, 22 * 40:1–14 (15–19), 54
Lamentations 3:1–9, 19–33
1 Peter 1:10–20
John 13:36–38 * John 19:38–42

*After these things, Joseph of Arimathea, who was
a disciple of Jesus, though a secret one . . . Nicodemus,
who had at first come to Jesus by night . . .*
JOHN 19:38–39

Both Joseph of Arimathea and Nicodemus are secret Christians. Some would dismiss their faith out of hand—where is the courage of their convictions? Aren't we supposed to shout our faith from the housetops?

Well, not many of the disciples are shouting on that Friday. Not any. Joseph and Nicodemus weren't the only ones afraid to come out—in fact, they were more able than the more open followers to come forward to claim his body, precisely because they had been less than open up until that day. They were important, well-respected members of the religious establishment, men whom the Romans knew. They could do what Peter and James could not.

And would not, in any case. Because Peter and James were nowhere to be found.

These powerful men could afford to concern themselves with the body of Jesus. And so could a few people at the other end of the power spectrum, the women around Jesus. They were free to act, like the two important leaders, but for the opposite reason: Nobody knew or cared what women did. What they did just didn't matter. Power and powerlessness, both perfect covers.

It's we in the middle. We who have a little power, a little security, and fear losing what we have. We are the ones who hide. But we don't get to see what's happening if we hide, don't get to be part of it. I guess that's why Jesus always said you have to lose your life in order to save it.

HOLY SATURDAY

Pss 95, 88 * 27
Lamentations 3:37–58
Hebrews 4:1–16
Romans 8:1–11

*My eyes cause me grief at the fate
of all the young women in my city.*
LAMENTATIONS 3:51

Of course, the writer is talking about the crime of rape, visited upon the women of an ancient conquered city. It is such a common part of the spoils of war that the writer can imagine it before it happens, because he knows it *will* happen.

Warfare is so different now: smart bombs, dirty bombs, night vision rifles, chemical weapons. But this ancient outrage has not changed: Humiliate the enemy by violating his women. Let there be a group of people whose lives and bodies have no worth, and let them be free for the taking. Let the act of love become a tool of hate.

War is the devil's playground. Everything is upside down: Your best friendships are right here, but they exist in an enterprise centered on killing. Your most courageous moment is here, and that moment plunges you into a horror that will never leave you, that waits for you to go to sleep so that it may visit in the night. Everything you hold dear is invoked as the reason you are here, but every moment holds the very real threat that you will never see any of it again.

And Jesus lies lifeless in his tomb, while war swirls in its endless circle just outside. Sometimes its cruelties are too much to bear. Sometimes we think we cannot endure another minute, that we have come to the end of our strength and the end of our hope. And maybe we have come to the end of *ours*.

But he stirs in the dark. Our hope in him is just beginning.